THE LORD'S PRAYER

REV. ROBERT ANDERSON

THE LORD'S PRAYER

OUR HEAVENLY MODEL FOR APPROACHING THE THRONE OF GOD

WHITAKER HOUSE

All Scripture quotations are taken from the King James Version of the Holy Bible.

The Lord's Prayer
Our Heavenly Model for Approaching the Throne of God

ISBN: 978-1-64123-790-1
eBook ISBN: 978-1-64123-791-8

Printed in the United States of America

Whitaker House
1030 Hunt Valley Circle
New Kensington, PA 15068
www.whitakerhouse.com

Library of Congress Control Number: 2021938448

1 2 3 4 5 6 7 8 9 10 11 28 27 26 25 24 23 22 21

"He who gave us the gift of life, taught us also the way of prayer. What prayer can be more spiritual than that which was given us by Christ, by whom the Holy Spirit was sent to us? What form of prayer can be more true in the sight of the Father than that which was delivered by the lips of His Son, who is Himself the Truth."

—*St. Cyprian* (200–258)
Bishop of Carthage

"We have received from the Lord a Rule of Prayer, which we must not transgress, either by adding to it or by leaving out any part of it. If you examine the words of all the prayers used by the saints, you will find nothing which the Lord's Prayer does not contain and bring within its compass. It is therefore at your choice to pray in different words from time to time, while you yet offer the same petitions in your prayers, but it must not be at your choice to offer different petitions. If we pray aright and agreeably to God's Word, we say nothing else than that which is included in the Lord's Prayer."

—*St. Augustine* (354–430)

CONTENTS

PREFACE

Our Lord has left this divine prayer with His church, not only as a model of all prayers, but also as an express form of words to be used by all the people of God as often as they approach the throne of grace. In obedience, therefore, to our Lord's command, the Church of England has introduced this prayer into all her services, both stated and occasional. It is placed, moreover, in the Church Catechism, accompanied by a paraphrase, which explains to children what they desire of God in this prayer. By our daily use of it, we realize, in its fullest sense, the communion of saints, seeing that the words of this prayer have been daily repeated by God's people in every age of the Christian church. Upon all these accounts, it is hoped that a plain, practical exposition of the Lord's Prayer will be regarded as a fit subject for a volume of the believer's library.

I will only add that I have endeavored to write this exposition in very simple language, such as may easily be understood by all classes of readers; and that, with the same view, I have occasionally made some verbal alterations in the various passages which I have extracted from the works of different authors, both ancient and modern, on the subject of the Lord's Prayer.

—*Rev. Robert Anderson*
Brighton, England (1840)

QUESTIONS AND ANSWERS FROM THE CHURCH CATECHISM

Question:

My good Child, know this; that thou art not able to do these things of thyself, nor to walk in the commandments of God, and to serve Him, without His special grace; which thou must learn at all times to call for by diligent prayer. Let me hear, therefore, if thou canst say the Lord's Prayer.

Answer:

Our Father, who art in heaven, hallowed be Thy name; Thy kingdom come; Thy will be done on earth, as it is in heaven. Give us this day our daily bread;

and forgive us our trespasses, as we forgive those who trespass against us. And lead us not into temptation, but deliver us from evil. Amen.

Question:

What desirest thou of God in this Prayer?

Answer:

I desire my Lord God, our heavenly Father, who is the giver of all goodness, to send His grace unto me, and to all people; that we may worship Him, serve Him, and obey Him, as we ought to do.

And I pray unto God that he will send us all things that are needful both for our souls and bodies; and that He will be merciful unto us, and forgive us our sins; and that it will please Him to save and defend us in all dangers both of soul and body; and that He will keep us from all sin and wickedness, and from our spiritual enemy, and from everlasting death. And this I trust He will do of his mercy and goodness, through our Lord Jesus Christ. And therefore I say, Amen, So be it.[1]

CHAPTER ONE

THE PETITION TO OUR FATHER WHICH IS IN HEAVEN, FOR THE HALLOWING OF HIS NAME

After this manner therefore pray ye: Our Father which art in heaven, hallowed be thy name.
—Matthew 6:9

And he said unto them, When ye pray, say, Our Father which art in heaven, hallowed be thy name.
—Luke 11:2

In the Lord's Prayer, we are furnished with a heavenly model of prayer[2] according to which all our devotions should be framed. For when Jesus Christ first delivered this prayer in His Sermon on the Mount, He said to His disciples, "*After this manner...pray ye*" (Matthew 6:9). But we are sure that our Lord intended it, not only as a pattern by which we are to regulate all our other prayers, but as an actual form of words, to be used exactly as they are here set down for our guidance in all our exercises of devotion; seeing that, when He delivered this prayer the second time, He introduced it with these words: "***When ye pray****, say, Our Father which art in heaven, hallowed be thy name*" (Luke 11:2). And this conclusion is fully supported by the circumstances which accompanied this second delivery of the prayer. For our Lord's disciples had just referred to a form of prayer, with which John the Baptist's disciples had been provided; and it was in answer to their request that He would teach them "*to pray, as John also taught his disciples*" (Luke 11:1) that Jesus left with His church this divine form of prayer, to be used by Christians in every age as the badge of their discipleship. Accordingly, we find it spoken of as "the daily prayer" by Saint Cyprian and others of the early fathers; and all the liturgies of the early Christian churches have it in every one of their services.

A Note on Disliking Prescribed Forms of Prayer

Now, if any of us have been accustomed to undervalue or dislike prescribed forms of prayer, as being apt, in our opinion, to degenerate into coldness or formality, we should remember that we have here a form of prayer actually prescribed by our

Lord Himself; and we should consider, therefore, whether the coldness and formality of which we complain may not be owing entirely to our own want of affection in spiritual things. For if we are always desiring variety in prayer, what is it but the want of a spiritual mind that makes this needful? In order that our affections may be lively in that holy exercise, we find it necessary that they should be continually stirred up by new expressions; whereas the soul that is really in earnest in the thing itself, for itself, panting ardently after the grace of God and the pardon of sin, regards not in what terms utterance shall be given to its petitions, whether new or old. Nay, though these petitions may be in the words which have been heard and uttered a thousand times, yet still they will be new to a spiritual mind. And, surely, the devotion that continues in lively exercise while pursuing this regular and constant path has more evidence of sincerity and true vigor in it than that which depends upon new notions and new words to move it, and which cannot, as it were, stir a step without them.

To borrow the language of the good Archbishop Leighton:

> We may well doubt whether that can be any other than a false flash of temporary devotion, which comes only by the power of some moving strain of prayer that is altogether new. But when confession of sin and requests for pardon, though uttered in accustomed terms, are found to carry the heart along with them heavenward, it is then far more certain that the Spirit of God dwelling in us, and the sense of the things themselves, such as the esteem of the blood of Christ, and the favour of God, really move the heart, since there is no novelty of words to help it.[3]

Let us not err, then, in a point of such importance as this; but let us rest assured that when the Holy Spirit teaches God's people to pray, He exercises His blessed influences not so much on the understanding as on the affections. Let us not suppose, therefore, that when He pours upon us the spirit of grace and supplication, His work consists, wholly or chiefly, in furnishing new supplies of thoughts and words; but let us consider it, rather, as His peculiar province to excite the heart anew at times of prayer, that so it may break forth in ardent desires to the Lord God of our salvation.

Following the guidance of Christian antiquity, the Church of England has introduced this divine prayer into all the various services in the prayer book, whether stated or occasional;[4] that so, by its perfection, it may, as it were, supply the defects of our own services, and may compensate for our own ignorance or blindness, in approaching the throne of grace. And, indeed, "though men should speak with the tongues of angels, yet words so pleasing to the ears of God, as these which the Son of God Himself hath composed, were not possible for men to frame."[5]

> He therefore which made us to live, hath also taught us to pray, to the end that speaking unto the Father in his Son's own prescript form...we may be sure that we utter nothing which God will either disallow or deny. Other prayers we use many besides this, but this oftener than any other....The causeless dislike thereof which others have conceived, is no sufficient reason for us as much as once to forbear, in any place, a thing which uttered with true devotion and zeal of heart, affordeth to God himself that glory, that aid to the

weakest sort of men, to the most perfect that solid comfort which is unspeakable.[6]

The Perfection of the Lord's Prayer

And, assuredly, the more we enter into the depth and fullness of this divine prayer, the more we shall feel disposed to doubt whether it can be too frequently repeated in the assemblies of the church. Our ignorance in asking is too gross to be denied; and it is too certain, moreover, that if our hearts do not accompany the words which we utter, our prayers will only be as mockery in God's sight. What, then, can be more wise or just or holy than, at short and frequent intervals, to recall to our minds both for what, and in what manner, we ought to pray, by the insertion of the Lord's Prayer, every clause of which is suited to recall the wandering heart, and whose fullness will supply every defect, since it tacitly implies, though it does not positively express, our desire for everything which man can wish or ought to ask? Superior[7] this prayer is in excellence, comprehensive in brevity, holy in substance, solemn in manner, and simple in expression; it is, at once, so short, that the meanest may learn it; so plain, that the most ignorant may understand it; and yet so full, that it comprehends all our wants and intimates all our duty, sheaving not only what is fit to be asked but what manner of persons we that ask ought to be. And well, therefore, might Tertullian speak of it as "the epitome of the gospel"; since it contains our persuasion of God's love, our desire of His honor, our subjection to His authority, our submission to His will, our dependence on His providence; together with our earnest supplication for mercy to deliver us from the guilt and for grace to deliver us from the power of sin; concluding with acts of faith and praise and adoration.

But, after all, who shall attempt to give dignity, by human praise, to that which proceeded from the Lord of all? It was He who spoke as never man spoke; it was Jesus, the wise, the holy, and the just, who gave this prayer for the use and imitation of His disciples; and, therefore, if we are not moved to adopt it by the reverence and gratitude which we feel for its Author, it were in vain to endeavor to influence the heart or the understanding by the weak applauses of a creature's tongue. They, and they only, whose hearts are touched with the flame of true devotion can value this prayer aright; and sure I am that no really devout worshipper of God will ever complain of the frequent repetition of such a prayer as this. For who, I would ask, ever finds it a wearisome task frequently to think or speak of that in which his heart is really engaged? Who does not find rather, that, in such case, the very recurrence of the term, which is expressive of the object so endeared to us, gives it the greater and more powerful access to his heart? Now, it is the heart, which is the only real seat of all true religion. It is upon this account that we are taught, by our church, to call upon the "Lord of all power and might," beseeching Him to "graft in our hearts the love of [His] Name."[8] And who that offers up such a petition in spirit and in truth can ever be weary of saying, *"Our Father which art in heaven,* ***hallowed be thy name****"* (Matthew 6:9)?

Praying "Our Father"

"Our Father," Not "*My Father*"

In teaching us to say not "my" but *"****our*** *Father,"* Jesus emphatically reminds us, not only that the prayer is suited as well for the purposes of public worship as for the daily use of every child of God, but also that our prayers, even when they are most private, should be charitably extended, so as to take in, with our own, the good of others; and that, when we are most earnest in offering prayers for ourselves at a throne of grace, we should not be unmindful of our brethren. Let the place and the performance of secret prayer be as private as may be; still we are here taught that the scope of our supplication should be public as well as personal. It follows, therefore, that the most private prayer of every true believer may be regarded as a public good; since the prayers which he pours forth may benefit others as well as himself. In like manner, every believer has a share in all the prayers of his brethren; and, in truth, though little considered by many of us, it is one of the many privileges belonging to that communion of saints that constitutes an article of our faith, that every believer participates in the prayers of the church at large. "He is a partner," says Archbishop Leighton, "in every ship of that kind that puts forth to sea; and he has a portion of all their gainful voyages." And, indeed, if the observation of Saint Ambrose be just, with regard to him "who prays for *himself alone*," namely, that he "stands *alone*, with no one else to pray for him," it is evident that even self-love may plead for this exercise of love to our brethren.

When engaged in the exercise of devotion, therefore, in our closets, let us not be unmindful of the church of God. Let us not forget to seek the good of Zion, seeing that it is not only our duty but that it may be our benefit so to do. For are we not all concerned in the good of Zion if we are, in truth, what we profess to be, parts of that mystical body of which Christ is the living Head? We find that David, even when lamenting his own sinfulness and praying for the light of God's countenance upon himself, was not unmindful of the church of God. "*Do good in thy good pleasure,*" he says, "*unto Zion: build thou the walls of Jerusalem*" (Psalm 51:18). And, assuredly, this should be the constant tenor of our prayers even in secret. "*When thou prayest,*" says Jesus, in the passage immediately preceding the first delivery of this prayer, "*shut thy door*" (Matthew 6:6). We are to shut out, therefore, as much as we can, the sight and notice of others; but we are not to shut out the interest and the good of others. Let us remember the words of the prophet Malachi: "*Have we not all one Father? Hath not one God created us?*" (Malachi 2:10); and let us say, with overflowing hearts, "*Our Father.*"[9]

Yes; let this be the spirit in which we daily utter these words, regarding ourselves as intercessors, one for another, because we are bound together by the tie of "one Communion and fellowship, in the mystical body of...Christ";[10] and then, how ardent will be our devotions when we assemble together on each returning Sabbath in the courts of the Lord's house! Having been accustomed, always, to regard ourselves and others as the members of that one mystical body, we shall never exhibit within the house of God, the listless countenance or the wandering eye, as if the exercise of public worship were nothing to us. But we shall rejoice at every new opportunity of entering the House of Common Prayer; and while, with a pure heart and humble voice, we repeat, each for himself and for all around him, the words "our Father,"[11] we shall experience something of that holy rapture which led the patriarch to exclaim, "*This is none other but the house of God, and this is the gate of heaven*" (Genesis 28:17).

The Father's Abhorrence of Sin

And now, as we pause for a while upon these words, "our Father," let us consider how forcibly they declare to us that, though love surpassing thought beams forth in every part of the great scheme of salvation, still it is a love in perfect consistency with a holiness which cannot look upon iniquity. It is, in short, the love of that almighty God, who has not exerted His omnipotence in silencing or overstepping the claims of justice, but in meeting them and fulfilling them. For before we can contemplate God as our Father, we must first regard Him as the Father of our Lord Jesus Christ, who yet became the Son of man, that He might make us the sons of God. Yes, though we know that Jesus Christ is that well-beloved Son, in whom the Father is always well pleased; though we know that the Father possessed Him *"in the beginning of his way, before his works of old"* (Proverbs 8:22); yet such is the Father's abhorrence of sin, that this well-beloved Son must humble Himself unto death, even the death of the cross, before the sinner can be redeemed from the curse which sin has introduced. To all, therefore, who refuse to honor this Son as the one appointed Mediator between God and man, God is and must be a consuming fire!

Sons of the Heavenly Father

"But as many as receive him, to them gave he power to become the sons of God" (John 1:12). And O, what heart can conceive, or what tongue can declare, the blessedness of those who are made *"the children of God by faith in Christ Jesus"* (Galatians 3:26)! Having been admitted at holy baptism into the family of God, they have deemed it their highest privilege to approach Him day by day in the words of this divine prayer, which was

then repeated in their behalf as a pledge of their adoption into the congregation of Christ's flock. Under all the trials and amidst all the changes of this mortal life, they have known what it is to look to their heavenly Father for guidance and for help. And if they have ever wandered from their Father's house, they have deeply felt what an evil and bitter thing it is thus to turn away from Him, of whom they can say that, from their own experience, He is not, as the world ignorantly conceives, a hard and severe taskmaster but a loving and tender Father, sparing us when we deserve punishment, and, in the midst of judgment, thinking upon mercy. May we ever hear that Father saying to us, *"How shall I put thee among the children, and give thee a pleasant land, a goodly heritage of the hosts of nations?"* (Jeremiah 3:19; see margin). And, with our hearts penetrated by a sense of such unutterable love, may we each of us have grace to say, *"My Father, thou art the guide of my youth"* (Jeremiah 3:4) and, "[I] *shalt not turn away from* [You]" (Jeremiah 3:19). For *"doubtless thou art our father, though Abraham be ignorant of us, and Israel acknowledge us not: thou, O Lord, art our father, our redeemer"* (Isaiah 63:16).

Let us, then, only ponder in our hearts the full scope and signification of the words *"Our Father which art in heaven"* (Matthew 6:9), and we shall feel constrained to say blessed and comprehensive forms of words![12] Almighty Father of all; Father of all that was and is and is to come; Father of everything that has, and everything that has not, within it the breath of life; Creator of the heavens and the earth; Creator of the angels, which excel in strength, and of all the host of heaven; Creator of all creatures that live and move and have their being upon the face of the earth; Creator of the fowls of the air and the fishes of the sea and the beasts of the field and creeping things innumerable; Creator of man; Father of our souls and our bodies; great Source of all we are and have and hope for; to You, the eternal Parent of the universe, we lift our thoughts, in the humility of prayer, when we bid our tongues obey the commands of Your Son and address You as "our Father!" Our Father Thou art, because You have formed us out of the dust of the ground; our Father Thou art, because You have adopted us into the children of Your inheritance; our Father, because You have spiritually begotten us, that we might be called the sons of God; our Father, because we are the brethren, and Thou art the very Father of our Lord Jesus Christ. In all these glorious attributes, and under all these varied forms of creation, we look up to You when we call on You as "our Father." You have graciously imparted to us that spirit of adoption, whereby we cry *"Abba, Father"* (Romans 8:15); and what is there which You will not vouchsafe in answer to the prayers of Your children, seeing that You have not denied them this, the greatest privilege of all, namely, to call You "Father"?

"Our father," too, *"which art in heaven"* (Matthew 6:9)! And, therefore, as heavenly and not as earthly do we call upon You.[13] Emboldened to address You as *"our father which art in heaven,"* we raise our thoughts from earth to heaven; we look up to that seat where Your host dwelt from eternity, enthroned in majesty above all height and clothed with light which no eye can bear to behold. To none upon earth do we call; for they, being earthly, could neither hear nor help us according to our wants. But You dwell above all as the King of Kings and the Lord of Lords in the height and in the holiness of heaven; You are a Spirit and, therefore, the discerner of our spirits; You are holy and, therefore, a lover

and rewarder of the holy; You are high and above all and, therefore, are able to look into the very inmost chambers of the heart, knowing all our necessities before we ask, and our ignorance in asking.

In teaching us to say *"our Father,"* our Lord reminds us of the mercy of Him, on whom we call, in order that He may beget in us the confidence of faith; and in teaching us to say *"our Father* ***which art in heaven,"*** He reminds us of His majesty, that He may beget in us humility and reverential fear. And it is in this mingled spirit of childlike confidence, deep humility, and holy fear that we should ever put forth our prayers to "our Father which is in heaven." For "most certain it is, that they who dare speak rashly to the God and Father of our Lord Jesus Christ know not His greatness; and that they who dare not speak to Him, provided it be with filial reverence and fear, know not His goodness."[14] Moreover, as often as the believer repeats the words *"our Father which art in heaven,"* he regards them as sealing to him the blessed assurance that his portion is *"in heaven"*; that his inheritance lies there, where it cannot be lost or impaired. And, therefore, if the believer deems it his best privilege to call God "Father," it is because he knows that to be the son of God is not an empty title; but that He who makes us "sons" makes us "heirs" likewise; even *"heirs of God, and joint-heirs with Christ"* (Romans 8:17). For although earthly fathers, by reason of the limited nature of all worldly possessions, are compelled, for the most part, to restrict their inheritance to their elder children, it is not thus with the possession which God has in store for those that love Him. No, all who belong to the family of God are partakers of the same rich inheritance; and all who are made *"to be partakers of the inheritance of the saints in light"* (Colossians 1:12) shall, as ages roll along, still stand beside the ocean of the divine perfections and shall still exclaim, with adoring hearts, "'*O the depth of the riches…of the wisdom*' (Romans 11:33) and power and love of our Father and our God!" It was to purchase this inheritance for us that the Son of God came from heaven to earth; and He is returned there to prepare it for us. "*I go,*" says Jesus to all true believers, "*to prepare a place for you….That where I am, there ye may be also*" (John 14:2–3).

Hallow His Name

Do we then desire to be "where He is"? If we do, let us show that we are continually mindful of our inheritance by "hallowing the name" of " our Father which is in heaven"; let us show that we are continually mindful of our inheritance, by walking as becomes the children of that Father who, while by making us "*joint-heirs with Christ,*" has given us a "*name better than of sons and of daughters*" (Isaiah 56:5), and has commanded us to show that we belong to His family by having our conversation daily in heaven. And let us consider, within ourselves, how certain it is that then only is God's name really hallowed by His children, when they are "*holy in all manner of conversation*" (1 Peter 1:15). For though we may tell the world that God is holy, they know Him not; they can neither see Him nor His holiness. But when they see that there are men of the same sinful and polluted nature with themselves, who are yet so renewed in the spirit of their minds that they hate the defilements of the world and do indeed live as burning and shining lights in the midst of a perverse and crooked generation; this may, and this will, convince them that there is, in a land far off, a spring of holiness, in all its blessed fullness, and from whence these drops have descended upon the children of men.[15]

And while we thus daily endeavor to hallow the name of our God in all our life and conversation, let our daily conviction of the weakness of our mortal nature, and of the imperfection of our best and holiest services, lead us daily to rejoice in the thought that there are purer services and praises given Him above; that there are multitudes of angels and glorified spirits hallowing and praising His great and glorious name, who *"rest not day and night, saying, Holy, holy, holy, LORD God Almighty, which was, and is, and is to come"* (Revelation 4:8). In this grand chorus, all the children of God, even though yet militant on earth, are permitted to take part. And we should therefore daily endeavor, by divine grace, so to live above the snares and temptations of this sinful world, that we may be able to add our joyful acclamation, saying, though in a lower key, in answer to the words of the heavenly worshippers, "Even so Lord, *'hallowed be thy name.'"*[16]

CHAPTER TWO

THE PETITION FOR THE COMING OF HIS KINGDOM

"Thy kingdom come."
—Matthew 6:10; Luke 11:2

The opening words of this divine prayer have taught us that our supplications at the throne of grace, even when they are most private, should be charitably extended to others; and that, when we are most earnest in offering up prayers for ourselves, we should not be unmindful of the wants of mankind at large; for we pray that "our heavenly Father's name may be hallowed." And can we utter this petition in sincerity and truth without desiring the continual increase of such devout worshippers, as may present this *"incense shall be offered unto my name, and a pure offering"* (Malachi 1:11)? In one word, can we daily pray that God's name may be hallowed without desiring that the kingdom of His grace may come in the fullness of its power and extent, and that *"the kingdoms of this world"* may *"become the kingdoms of our Lord, and of his Christ"* (Revelation 11:15)?

When we consider the state of things at the time when the kingdom of God, or the gospel dispensation, was first "coming," or approaching among men, we may regard our Lord's disciples as desiring that, in the first instance, Christianity might soon be propagated through the world; so that all men might willingly acknowledge God as their Lord and Maker, worshipping and serving Him in truth; and that they might receive His blessed Son Jesus Christ as their King and Savior, heartily embracing His doctrines and humbly submitting to His laws. And, by parity of reason, as we utter this clause in the Lord's Prayer, we should desire that the Christian religion may be settled and confirmed, may grow and increase, and may prosper and flourish in the world; that God's authority may be maintained and promoted both in external profession and real effect; the minds of all men being subdued to the obedience of faith, freely and cheerfully avowing the subjection due to Him, and truly yielding obedience to His most just and holy laws. And it is in the spirit of this divine prayer, therefore, that our own scriptural Collect, for all "conditions of men," opens with an earnest petition to God as the "Creator and Preserver of all mankind," beseeching Him, "that [He] wouldest be pleased to make [His] ways known unto them, [His] saving health unto all nations."[17]

The Kingdom of God in Our Hearts

On the other hand, unless we ourselves, who utter this prayer, shall receive the kingdom of God into our own hearts, to what purpose do we pray to Him, as if we desired that it should be enlarged and flourish abroad? Accordingly, in the Collect just referred to, we go on to pray for ourselves, who are the subjects of that kingdom, beseeching God to grant that we "who profess and call [ourselves] Christians may be led into the way of truth, and hold the faith in unity of spirit, in the bond of peace, and in righteousness of life."[18] And, in like manner, as often as we pray in the words "Thy kingdom come" for the gradual enlargement and future perfection of God's visible kingdom, we must remember that, unless, at such seasons of prayer, we are trifling with the divine Majesty, we are thus beseeching our heavenly Father, that He would graciously establish His kingdom in our own hearts. This personal application of the prayer to our own hearts and lives, it behooves each of us to regard, as we daily utter the words of this clause. And, keeping this in view, I know not how I can better illustrate this clause in the Lord's Prayer than by our Lord's answer to the Pharisees when interrogated by them as to the coming of the kingdom of God.

> [Jesus] *answered them and said, The kingdom of God cometh not with observation: neither shall they say, Lo, here! or Lo, there! for, behold, the kingdom of God is within you.* (Luke 17:20–21)

As Jesus declares in these words, the kingdom of God is not in the pomp or the glory of the world. In vain shall we look for it there. Many there are who profess to desire it, but they will not learn how to look for it or how to prepare themselves for it. The search must be without cease; the preparation must be going on at every moment of our lives. Worldly men, dazzled by the glare of an earthly monarchy, are quite unable to discern the kingdom of God; and they care not to seek for it, since it is established only on the ruins of that love which they cherish for the world, and for the things belonging to it. The kingdom of grace is visible only to those who are endowed with spiritual discernment, and to whom the things that are not seen are their all in all.

But it may, perhaps, be lawful for us to consider the phrase "the kingdom of God within us" more particularly since our Lord's words were addressed to the Pharisees, as placed in contrast not only with outward pomp and splendor, generally, but, more especially, with the rites and solemnities which distinguished the worship of God under the law; and I would therefore offer a few remarks on the points of agreement and difference between the Mosaic and Christian dispensations.[19]

The Agreement of the Mosaic and Christian Dispensations

I will begin with their agreement. A very little consideration may induce us to accept the statement of the seventh article of our church, that "the Old Testament is not contrary to the New," but that "both in the Old and New Testament everlasting life is offered to mankind by Christ, who is the only Mediator between God and man."[20] The appointment of institutions adapted to the state and necessities of man for a season, and their repeal afterward, when they had fulfilled the purpose intended—this is consistent with every notion which we can form of perfect wisdom. But the will of the Almighty we cannot suppose subject to change; *"heaven and earth shall pass away,"* but the Word which God has spoken *"shall not pass away"* (Matthew 24:35). And, therefore, admitting the New Testament to be true, and embracing it as such, we cannot do otherwise than admit that, as a truth involved in this, the substance of the elder must be, in effect, one and the same with that of the later dispensation.

This point may be illustrated by comparing our Savior's declaration of giving His disciples *"a new commandment"* (John 13:34) with John's declaration *"Brethren, I write no new commandment unto you, but an old commandment which ye had from the beginning"* (1 John 2:7). It was a new commandment, then, not in letter or in effect, but in extent and sanction; new, in revealed motives, since it was founded now upon better promises; new, in respect of the example set for its fulfillment, and the encouragement offered for observing it; new, also, by reason of the practical degradation and disuse into which it had fallen. But, in purpose and effect, it was old; in respect of its inherent tendency to bring man into present happiness and peace, and to fit him for a blessed eternity, it was "the same which was from the beginning."

And not only has this great scheme of moral government been one in substance, but it has been uniformly working its way, so to speak, through the same substantial state of things. It has had to operate upon the same moral constitution of human nature; and it has had to travel onward through the same order of natural providences. Day unto day still uttered speech, and night unto night still showed knowledge: the lights of heaven still rule in the firmament; and seedtime and harvest, cold and heat, and summer and winter still return, as they always have returned, and as the Lord has declared that they always shall return, while the earth remains. Man, too, continues the same as ever—born with the same nature, tempted by the same passions, liable to fall continually through the same licentiousness of an obstinate will, and only to be restored by the same heavenly grace. Had it been otherwise, and had the laws of the divine government appeared subject to change or caprice, we might have doubted; but, as things are, from the very fact of their consistency, we are willing to believe that the same *"Lord God omnipotent reigneth"* (Revelation 19:6) over the children of men.

The Difference of the Mosaic and Christian Dispensations

But still there is a great difference between the Mosaic and Christian dispensations; and this may be illustrated by what Paul says in his epistle to the Galatians:

> *We, when we were children, were in bondage under the elements* [or *"rudiments"* (Colossians 2:8, 20)] *of the world: but when the fulness of the time was come, God sent forth his Son, made of a woman, made under the law, to redeem them that were under the law, that we might receive the adoption of sons.... Wherefore, thou art no more a servant, but a son; and if a son, then an heir of God through Christ.* (Galatians 4:3–7)

Under the Mosaic covenant, therefore, that appeal was chiefly made which was proportioned and adapted to the capacities of children. An open and direct appeal to the motives, the hopes, and the faculties, which belong to the more mature age, was reserved until the *"ministration of death"* and *"condemnation"* (2 Corinthians 3:7, 9), put to proof and found wanting, might itself stand forth, in its wreck and insufficiency, an additional and most convincing argument, that to live by sight is not the way to conquer the perverse will, nor to bring the heart of man unto that extent of obedience and purity, of which, even in this present life, God has vouchsafed to make it capable.

Such would appear to be the respective characters of these two dispensations; and, accordingly, the means employed under each will appear to be exactly adapted to the difference here pointed out in their several methods of appeal. In the earlier dispensation, we observe many splendid outward manifestations, by visible symbols of the divine presence, and by signs of guidance and protection, held forth to the very eyesight of the subjects whom it called to body: but only a temporary end was fully declared. The real and enduring end was hidden, as it were, behind a veil. Under the gospel, the order is reversed. As the glory of the latter revelation infinitely surpasses that of the former, yet, like the latter compared with the former temple, it is greater only by a spiritual greatness. The law may be truly said to have had its end veiled, with its means of appeal outward and visible; whereas the gospel, or the kingdom of grace, has its means inward and spiritual but its end fully revealed.

The Three Christian Graces

The view which we have now been taking of the Christian dispensation, as not coming with observation or outward show but as being the kingdom or reign of God within us, is calculated under the divine blessing to promote the growth of the three Christian graces so peculiarly characteristic of a spiritual kingdom—faith, hope, and love.

Faith

The first is faith. Viewing ourselves as the subjects of a spiritual dispensation, we shall not stagger through unbelief at the mournful sight which is so continually presented to us by the two opposite classes of practical and intellectual unbelievers. For we shall well know the hopelessness of expecting to convert or convince, by merely human means, those who will persist in strengthening themselves in the might and the pride of their own unassisted understanding. We shall feel within ourselves a living witness that it is not by our own strength that we stand but by the grace and blessing of God upon the disposition which He has given us to receive His will. If we would habitually view ourselves in this light, we should learn how to conduct ourselves toward persons betraying either of these unhappy states of mind; ever remembering that, while we must keep fast to our own convictions, as we value our immortal souls, we must, at the same time, prove the sincerity and power of those convictions by abounding more and more in the fruits of patience, forbearance, meekness, and gentleness to all around us; and must ever remember that the strength of the believer lies in internal confidence, not in outward debate and strife. All are not warriors and champions in the Israel of God. Many cannot go forth with the armor of disputation; for they have not proved it. But all who surely trust in the protection of God, who has preserved the heritage and flock of their fathers, may wield successfully the sling and the stone of a simple and charitable conversation. And that which is prescribed to Christians, generally, in this matter, is to be ready to give a reason of the hope that is in them with meekness and fear, and with well-doing to put to silence the ignorance of foolish men.

Hope

We see how the subject before us bears upon the cultivation of the grace of hope. By hope, I would here be understood to comprehend, in its fullest sense, not only an assured expectation of an eternal state of glory and joy but that state of mind ascribed to the father of the faithful, which *"against hope* [can believe] *in hope"* (Romans 4:18), such as in contemplating the general aspects of a fallen world.

It may be said of the believer that he *"casts* [his] *bread upon the waters"* only in the sure hope of *"find*[ing] *it after many days"* (Ecclesiastes 11:1). Always bearing in mind that the kingdom of God comes not with outward show, he derives comfort from the assurance that, upon that very account, they who belong to that heavenly kingdom and are fellow citizens with the saints care not to have their works seen of men, or to have men say, *"Lo here! or, Lo there!"* (Luke 17:21), but are content to tread in secret the path of duty, with a conscience void of offense toward God and toward man. He knows that the spiritual fabric, which is erected on the basis of faith and love, and of which Jesus Christ is the chief cornerstone, generally rises in secrecy and silence toward the gates of heaven; and that it may be said of it, as of the temple of Jerusalem of old, that there is *"neither hammer nor axe nor any tool of iron heard in the house, while it* [is] *in building"* (1 Kings 6:7). Remembering this, amidst appearances the most discouraging, the believer still looks up to the polar-star of Christian hope. It may be that, in the mercy of God, he shall find the bread which he has cast upon the waters in this life, but he reckons upon it only in another. The believer does not look, therefore, toward the visible sum of other people's account but to that which serves toward the positive increase, the required amount of his own. He knows that he is to "*work out* [his] *own salvation with fear and trembling*" (Philippians 2:12); and, in this, he is always upheld by a hope which make not ashamed, because he knows also that "*it is God which worketh in* [him] *both to will and to do of his good pleasure*" (Philippians 2:13).

Love

But, in fulfilling this, his appointed work, the believer's path lies through the blessed employment of advancing the happiness of his fellow creatures. On this, therefore, the attention of the believer will always be set; and to this object he will, in the unwearied exercise of Christian love, be continually pressing forward. Not that he ever allows himself to form any wild or extravagant project of a universal reformation; but he desires, in simplicity and godly sincerity, to contribute his own share toward an event which he is satisfied to leave in the hands of the Almighty. And, with this end always in view, he humbly endeavors, at all times and in all ways, to recommend that which is good to others by the light of personal example; so that they, who will not listen to the words, may be brought to reverence the works of the Spirit and be led at last to "*glorify* [our] *father which is in heaven*" (Matthew 5:16).

Let it thus be seen from the manner in which we walk before men that the kingdom of God is indeed within us; let it only be seen that the whole complexion of our lives corresponds with the language of our prayers. Many of those who have been hitherto wandering in the ways of their own hearts will desire to become the subjects of that kingdom which begins on earth and is to be perfected in heaven.

For, be it remembered, the "kingdom" for the "coming" of which we daily pray is a kingdom to be *perfected* hereafter. Those members of the church who are already in heaven are permitted to witness, even now, some of its glorious manifestations. There is the throne of God especially established; and there it is that He displays Himself in the splendor of His majesty. In that blest abode, there is no mixture of the good and the bad together, neither is there any mixture of bad in the good; but all are holy, for *"there shall in no wise enter into it any thing that defileth"* (Revelation 21:27). There are neither temptations to try God's people nor sins to defile them nor sorrows to afflict them; but all is peace and purity and joy. For there, all tears have been wiped away from the eyes of its inhabitants; and all sin, the cause of those tears, has been rooted out of their hearts.

The Elements That Will Complete the Happiness of Saints

And yet, as it has been truly said, two things are still wanting to complete the happiness of the saints in heaven.

The Perfection of the Saints

For, on the one hand, the kingdom of God is not yet perfected; nor will it be, till the whole number of the elect shall be called, and the whole number of the called glorified. Many are yet conflicting here below, and ripening for their eternal reward, and many are yet unborn; all of whom God will, in His due time, bring into the possession of His heavenly kingdom to complete the number of His glorious subjects. And, therefore, it is said, concerning the saints who are already in heaven, that "*white robes were given unto every one of them; and it was said unto them, that they should rest yet for a little season, until their fellowservants also and their brethren...should be fulfilled*" (Revelation 6:11).

The Abolition of the Power of the Grave

And, on the other hand, those saints who are now in heaven have not attained to a perfect consummation of happiness because their bodies continue still under the arrest of death and the power of the grave. But, through that mysterious union which subsists between Jesus Christ and His mystical body, they shall, at His coming, obtain a glorious and joyful resurrection. And then shall the kingdom for which we pray be every way perfect. The kingdom shall itself be perfect in the full number of its subjects, and every subject shall be perfect, in his full reward—his soul made forever blessed in the blissful vision of God, and his body made inconceivably glorious by "*bear*[ing] *the image of the heavenly*" (1 Corinthians 15:49)—and both shall remain forever with the Lord.

May this hope animate our prayers; and, while thus engaged, we shall enjoy the blessedness of the communion of saints in its fullest extent. For though we may not pray to or for the souls of the departed, yet we may, and we should, pray with them for the second advent of Christ in His glorious majesty to judge the quick and dead. The souls of the faithful are, indeed, already "delivered from the burden of the flesh" and "are in joy and felicity."[21]

But as *"without us,"* they cannot be *"made perfect"* (Hebrews 11:40); so, together with us, they are looking forward to that day when all the redeemed of the Lord shall have their "perfect consummation and bliss, both in body and soul, in [His] eternal and everlasting glory."[22] Yes; in this we are permitted, even now, to join daily and hourly with the members of the church in heaven; namely, in praying that the days of sin and misery may be shortened; that Christ may come in His glory;[23] and that, after rising to the life immortal, we *all may be one,* Christ in us, and we in Christ, that we may be made *perfect in one.*

Amen. Even so, come, Lord Jesus. (Revelation 22:20)

CHAPTER THREE

THE PETITION FOR THE FULFILLMENT OF HIS WILL IN EARTH, AS IT IS FULFILLED IN HEAVEN

"Thy will be done in earth, as it is in heaven."
—Matthew 6:10

"Thy will be done, as in heaven, so in earth."
—Luke 11:2

As we proceed with this divine prayer, we perceive more and more clearly how suited it is to guide and assist us in ordering the frames and desires of the heart as often as we approach "our Father which is in heaven." We are plainly taught in it, not only to prefer the honor of God to our own immediate interest and to set the heart first upon its advancement, but to keep the heart steadfastly fixed on that one end. For the prayer leads us to dwell upon the honor due to the divine Majesty in three several petitions, thus...

> varying the expression of that one desire, as often as there be several requests following of our own concernment; teaching us that that doth, in its own worth, and therefore should likewise in our affection...[outweigh] all the different things besides that we can desire.[24]

And that one thing we should desire is that "Thy name be hallowed; Thy kingdom come; Thy will be done in earth, as it is in heaven."[25]

And not only does the dignity of the thing itself demand this adding of one request to another, in order to stir up our dull and backward affections to the pitch of true devotion, but as Archbishop Leighton remarks, there is, in the petitions themselves, a very profitable difference, though their scope be one. They are so many different arrows aimed at the same mark. In the first petition, *"Hallowed be thy name,"* we express our desire that every kind and degree of honor may be offered to the name of God. And because His name is especially honored in the advancement of His spiritual kingdom, the second petition is, *"Thy kingdom come."* And because, until that kingdom shall be completed, it lies in two several countries—the one part of it being already above, which is the appointed place for the perfection and perpetuity of this kingdom; the other part being here below, but continually tending thither—the words of this third petition, *"Thy will be done in earth, as it is in heaven,"* particularly relate to all who are serving God on earth; desiring that, in obedience to their King, they may be as much conformed as is possible to those who are serving Him above; even to those countless hosts of ministering spirits, who encircle His throne and who cease not day and night to celebrate and to serve Him with uninterrupted praises and with unerring obedience.[26]

The School of Obedience and Submission to God's Will

It follows, therefore, from the scope of this petition, that we ought to regard the world as a school in which we are to be taught obedience and submission to the will of God, so that we may be trained up for *"the inheritance of the saints in light"* (Colossians 1:12). For here it is that we discover the necessity of God's government and the equity and excellence of God's law. Here it is that we learn the indispensable obligation of full and unreserved submission to God's will; seeing that misery, discord, and confusion arise from the opposition of human wills and their perpetual struggles for the mastery. And here it is that we learn to prize that holy reverential fear of God which is the source of all true obedience; seeing that they only are able, at all times and under all circumstances, to *"delight themselves in the abundance of peace"* (Psalm 37:11), whose hearts are filled with this spirit of holy fear, and whose feet have therefore been guided into all the paths of such obedience.

But if this be the lesson which the Christian may derive from his residence in the world, how sweet and how abundant is the encouragement which he receives in every part of Scripture, thus to persevere in his obedience! "*What man is he that feareth the* L*ORD*? *him shall he teach*," says David, "*in the way that he shall choose*" (Psalm 25:12). Yea, says a greater than David, "*If any man will do his will, he shall know of the doctrine, whether it be of God, or whether I speak of myself*" (John 7:17). And, to represent still more emphatically the Christian's privileges, our Lord says elsewhere, "*Whosoever shall do the will of God, the same is my brother, and my sister, and mother*" (Mark 3:35). In other words, the man who does the will of God from the heart does, in very deed, belong to the family and household of God. For, by "keeping the words" of Jesus, the believer shows that he "loves Him" (see John 14:15); and of everyone who thus loves Him and keeps His words, Jesus says, "*My Father will love him, and we will come unto him, and make our abode with him*" (John 14:23). Such is the gracious promise which the Savior has made to all who walk in the way of God's commandments; and well, therefore, may all such be described as...

The living homes where Christ shall dwell,
And never pass away.[27]

The Petition "Thy Will Be Done"

With such encouragements before us, let us now turn to the petition which our Lord Himself has taught us to use, and let us ponder in our hearts the full scope of these few but comprehensive words: *"Thy will be done in earth, as it is in heaven"* (Matthew 6:10).

Now, what is the spirit in which we usually repeat the words *"thy will be done"*? When we utter this petition, is it in the spirit of simple acquiescence in our heavenly Father's will? Do we, in short, view God as a kind and tender and compassionate Parent, sparing us when we deserve punishment and, in the midst of judgment, thinking upon mercy? And do we, therefore, desire to improve the talents committed to our charge, in conformity with the will of Him whose we are and whom we ought to serve with every faculty and every affection of the soul? Or do we not, rather, too frequently hide our talent in a napkin or conceal it under the earth, like the slothful servant in the parable, as if we were called upon to serve an austere master, who would compel us to serve with rigor and would make our lives bitter with hard bondage?

Yes; we are all too apt either to worship altogether a god of our own imagination or to form our judgment of the character of God only from that unwilling exercise of His severer attributes, which we have, as it were, extorted from Him by our sins. But if we would view the Lord our God, not in this partial light, nor according to the vain and shallow and imperfect conceptions of our own corrupt and ignorant minds, but as He is plainly revealed to us in the Bible, in all the glorious harmony of the divine perfections, we should at once feel and acknowledge that even *"as a father pitieth his children, so the* L*ORD* *pitieth them that fear Him"* (Psalm 103:13). We should there find it written in every page that, though we have left our Father's house and have been blindly following the devices and desires of our own sinful hearts, He is still stretching forth His hands to us and promising us forgiveness of all that is past if, with a perfect and true heart, we will return unto Him. Let us, therefore, acquaint ourselves with the character and dispensations of God as set forth in Scripture; and we shall understand that, when He calls upon us to "do His will," or, in other words, to be holy, even as He is holy, He does, in effect, call upon us to be happy, even as He is happy. In one word, let us only return to our Father's house; and, in proportion as we shall exchange the miserable bondage of sin and Satan for that service of God in which our freedom consists, we shall find that the holiness in which we are now commanded to walk is only another name for happiness commenced upon earth; being, as it were, a pledge to assure us that the perfection of happiness which awaits us hereafter is only the perfection of holiness in the kingdom of the blessed.

"Our will," says Bishop Lancelot Andrewes,

> is blind and foolish; but God's will is full of counsel and wisdom. Our will is crooked and perverse and froward; but His will is full of all goodness, which we are to understand hereby, that He showeth Himself a Father to us. If a child be left to his own will, it is as much as his life is worth; and our will being childish, we must be abridged of it, or else we shall fall into danger. Therefore do we pray not only that we may submit our will to God's, but that we may utterly deny our own will, so that God's holy will may take place in us. Nor is this all: we pray not only that we may have a will and desire to do God's will, but also that we may have ability and power to do it, since, of ourselves, we have no strength for the performance.

The apostle saith that we are not sufficient of ourselves to think a good thought. (See 2 Corinthians 3:5.) Yea, such is our corruption, that though God will, yet we will not. It is certain, then, that we have not of ourselves either will or ability, but that it is God who giveth both. Therefore, we are petitioners for the grace of God and for power from Him; so that our desire is to obtain something from God whereby His will may be accomplished in us. For, observe, it is not said, "Let us do," or, "Do Thou Thy will"; but, "Thy will be done." Then we must have that active grace by which the will of God may be done in us, according to the words of the prophet: *"Lord, thou… hast wrought all our works in us"* (Isaiah 26:12). Yes; God must not only heal our thoughts and change our affections, but He must also bring to pass that, as He gives us ability to do His will, so His will may indeed be done by us. We must say with the psalmist, *"Thou hast been my help; leave me not, neither forsake me, O God of my salvation"* (Psalm 27:9). And with an earnest desire for the full performance of the divine will, we must daily say, with Christ, *"Not my will, but thine, be done"* (Luke 22:42); gladly abridging ourselves of our own will, that God's will may take place.[28]

God's Will "Done in Earth, as It Is in Heaven"

With such a view of the nature, the extent, and the blessedness of true and faithful obedience, let us now consider what is the full scope of our supplication when we pray that the will of our heavenly Father may be *"done in earth, as it is in heaven."*

I remember to have heard that, when the question "How is the will of God done in heaven?" was once put, the answer was made, "It is done by the angels in heaven immediately, diligently, always, altogether, with all their strength, and *without asking any questions about it."* And our answer would be in substance the same if, with Archbishop Leighton, we were to describe the obedience practiced in heaven as being a *cheerful* and *universal* obedience.

A Cheerful Obedience

The obedience of the angels in heaven is a cheerful obedience. The psalmist, after describing the angels of the Lord as "excelling in strength," immediately adds that they *"do his commandments, hearkening unto the voice of his word"* (Psalm 103:20). And from the connection, therefore, in which these words are placed, we find that the "strength" in which the angels "excel" is in continually performing the will of God. For it seems that the angels are endued with such excellent strength for this one end, namely, that they may *"do his commandments."*

In like manner, the Christian must devote all his strength to the fulfillment of God's commandments; and he will always experience the most inward joy and gladness when he keeps the closest to the divine will. For the law of God is not to him, as it is to others, a force from without, urging him on violently against his own rebellious will; but it is a power lodged within his heart, inclining and enabling him to pursue the path of God's commandments. As, therefore, he increases in strength, he will run with fresh alacrity the way of these commandments; and he will partake more largely of the blessedness of those *"whose strength is in thee, and in whose heart are the ways of them"* (Psalm 84:5). Not only are the feet of God's children in His ways, but, as the psalmist here declares, "His ways are in their hearts."

A Universal Obedience

The obedience of the angels in heaven is also universal. For in the same passage in which the angels are described as those who *"excel in strength,"* and who *"do his commandments,"* it is beautifully said of them that they *"hearken…unto the voice of his word"* (Psalm 103:20). The angels never turn away their ears from any, the least, of God's commandments. They wait but for a word from Him, and that is enough for them. And, in like manner, the true Christian will desire to *"have respect unto all* [God's] *commandments"* (Psalm 119:6) and to *"set the Lord always before* [him]" (Psalm 16:8) in a uniform, constant regard to His will. He will offer up his heart to God, that it may be fashioned and molded by Him to His will. He will desire to resign it up to his Lord and to be himself as a piece of wax in God's hand, ready to be molded to what form He will. His prayer will be that the Lord God would banish from his breast whatever may be displeasing in His sight, and that He would fill it with His good Spirit. It will be his constant desire that he may have no will but God's and that he may be altogether subject both to His commanding and to His disposing will,[29] being always prepared to do what He commands; and in all His dealings with us, to be pleased with what He does.

In one word, the language of the believer will be: "For my actions, let God's Word be my guide; and for the events of things, and all that concerns me, let His good pleasure and His wise disposal be my will. Yea, let me give up the rudder of my life into His hand, to be steered by Him into the haven of everlasting rest. And amidst all the changes of this lower world, let me have grace to say from my heart, *'My father, thou art the guide of my youth'* (Jeremiah 3:4); let me never *'turn away from* [Thee]' (verse 19)."

Such, then, is the mark at which we are commanded to aim; namely, an obedience to God's will, as cheerful and as universal as that of the angels which are about His throne. This is the high and unalterable standard by which we are to measure all our performances; this is the true scope which we profess to set before us, as often as we repeat the words of the petition *"Thy will be done in earth, as it is in heaven"* (Matthew 6:10)!

But, as we would hope really to transcribe these words into our hearts and lives, we must now endeavor, in conclusion, to fix our thoughts and our affections upon that Lamb of God, without blemish and without spot, of whom the Scriptures declare that He came to do the will of the Father. (See John 6:38.)[30]

Let us, then, in the first place, look to Jesus as having tabernacled among the children of men; and as we dwell on every part of His mysterious sufferings, let us regard them as declaring to us, with a voice which cannot be misunderstood, the gracious nature of that divine will, to which we pray that we may be conformed. For when the Son of God emptied Himself of all His glory in obedience to the Father's will, that

He might take our nature upon Him and suffer death for us upon the cross, then was it seen how justice and mercy met together to accomplish God's wonderful scheme of salvation for a rebellious world; then was it seen how the Son of God had been ordained to lift a load from the creation, under which it would otherwise have sunk into utter and endless ruin.

And when the view of our Savior's passion shall have deeply affected our hearts with a sense of the good will of that heavenly Father, who, to show His hatred for sin, coupled with the most tender compassion for the person of the sinner, *"spared not his own Son, but delivered him up for us all"* (Romans 8:32); when we shall have learned, from the great mystery of our redemption, how, in testimony of this good will to man, God *"hath made him to be sin for us, who knew no sin; that we might be made the righteousness of God in him"* (2 Corinthians 5:21); then let us lift up our hearts, in holy meditation, toward that temple above, even heaven itself, into which our High Priest is entered, *"now to appear in the presence of God for us"* (Hebrews 9:24); and let us ask, in His name, for such supplies of grace as may enable us to "do our Father's will in earth, as it is in heaven." For the Son of God came, not only to atone for the sins of men and to bring in everlasting righteousness for the justification of their persons, but also to bestow upon them a new and regenerate life, enabling them cheerfully and unreservedly to run the way of God's commandments.

Who but He who lives and reigns with the Father in the unity of the Holy Spirit; who but the Son of God could obtain for us help to guide our wandering feet into the paths of holiness and peace? Who but the Son of God could thus obtain for us grace to subdue our perverse and rebellious wins and to write all God's laws in our hearts? For, ever since the fall of Adam, man has been so enslaved by that carnal mind which is enmity against God, that, if left to himself, he would actually refuse to be made whole. Though light be come into the world, man would, if left to himself, still love darkness rather than light, and would not come to the Physician of souls, that he might be healed.

But, blessed be God, we have to do with a High Priest, of whom it was expressly written, He should make His people *"willing in the day of thy power"* (Psalm 110:3). Therefore, all who desire to do the will of God *"in earth, as it is in heaven"* will *"put…on the Lord Jesus Christ"* (Romans 13:14) as *"The Lord Our Righteousness"* (Jeremiah 23:6). They will put Him on as their perfect and everlasting righteousness for the justification of their persons; and they will put Him on as the all-sufficient source of righteousness and holiness for the inward sanctification of their hearts. They will pray that the Spirit which is derived from Him may so change them into the same divine image, that they may, in very deed, exchange that carnal mind which is enmity against God for that spiritual mind which is life and joy and peace; that they may be very members incorporate in that mystical body, of which Christ is the Head. If that prayer be answered, they will know what it is to do the will of God *"in earth, as it is in heaven."* For, if it be true that the mystical Head "came to do His Father's will" (see John 6:38), that He "delights to do it" (see Psalm 40:8), and that "the Father's law is within His heart" (see verse 8), assuredly He will so write it, by His Spirit, in the hearts of all His faithful people, that, as the members of His body, it will be their chief desire and their highest privilege to be, to do, and to suffer whatever their heavenly Father shall appoint.

Hear us, therefore, blessed Jesus, from Thy throne of grace, and so mold our hearts by Thy Holy Spirit, that we may indeed be enabled to do the will of Thy Father, and our Father *"in earth,"* even *"as it is in heaven"*!

> Write in our hearts what our heavenly Father commands us to do; and then let Him command what He will.[31]

Suffer us not to utter the words "God's will be done" with the slavish spirit of those who feel that they must submit only because they dare not offer any resistance to His will. But so shed abroad in our hearts the love of Him whose will we are commanded to do, that we may utter the words "Thy will be done" as dear children in the spirit of adoption, deeming it our best and greatest privilege to be always employed in fulfilling the will of God Himself by crucifying the flesh with the affections and lusts, and by abounding in every good word and work! And, to this end, be pleased, O Lord, so to mortify our hearts and all our members from all worldly and carnal lusts, that, whether it be by active obedience to the word or by a cheerful acquiescence in the providential appointments of our heavenly Father, we may, in all things, obey His blessed will and glorify His holy name! Amen! Amen!

CHAPTER FOUR

THE PETITION FOR DAILY BREAD

"Give us this day our daily bread."
—Matthew 6:11

"Give us day by day
[or "*for the day*" (marginal reading)] *our daily bread."*
—Luke 11:3

We have been instructed to pray to "our Father which is in heaven," so that "His name may be hallowed," "His kingdom may come," and "His will may be done in earth, as it is in heaven." And, when we have thus fulfilled our first and highest duty in praying for those things which pertain to the glory of God and the extension of His kingdom upon earth, then, and not till then, are we authorized to turn our views to those things which pertain to our bodies and this present life. When we have said from the bottom of our hearts, *"Our Father which art in heaven, Hallowed be thy name. Thy kingdom come, thy will be done in earth, as it is in heaven"* (Matthew 6:9–10), then, and not till then, are we permitted to utter a petition for the food by which our bodies live, that we may subsist. Then, and not till then, do we say, *"Give us this day our daily bread"* (verse 11); or, as it is in the eleventh chapter of Luke, *"Give us day by day* [or *"for the day"* (marginal reading)] *our daily bread."*[32]

The Temporal and Bodily Wants of Man

Now, limited and moderate as this petition is, it is yet the only petition of the Lord's Prayer which at all refers to the supply of the temporal and bodily wants of man. The rest of the prayer is altogether employed in making petitions for the concerns of the soul and eternity. Perhaps there is no other method by which we could have been so clearly and forcibly impressed with the judgment of our Lord upon the comparative value and importance of the present and the future world. For, while the life that now is, is touched upon by Him but slightly and but once; the world that is to come forms the groundwork of the whole prayer.

The Lessons We Learn from This Petition

Sobriety and Temperance

Commentators have remarked that every word of this petition—"*Give us this day*" (Matthew 6:11), or "*day by day our daily bread*" (Luke 11:3)—has a lesson for our instruction. We ask for bread, not for dainties or superfluities, but only for bread—only for what is needful for the body and for the support of those who depend upon us.[33] This teaches us sobriety and temperance.

Honesty and Industry

We ask for "our bread"; we do not ask for the "*bread of deceit*" (Proverbs 20:17) or the "*bread of idleness*" (Proverbs 31:27) but for bread honestly and lawfully gotten. This plainly teaches us honesty and industry.

Trusting in God's Providential Care

We ask for our "*daily bread.*"[34] In other words,[35] we ask for that which is sufficient for our daily life; we ask for what will strengthen us from day to day for serving God with cheerfulness and vigor. And this, therefore, emphatically teaches us not to take any anxious "*thought for the morrow*" (Matthew 6:34) but to live from day to day under a continual and growing sense of God's providential care.[36]

Asking God's Blessing on Our Food

Again, whatever may be our state or condition in life—whether high or low, rich or poor—we call upon God to "*give us day by day our daily bread,*" thereby acknowledging this important truth, namely, that the highest as well as the lowest of men must be beholden to the mercy of God for their daily food; and, above all, that they must be beholden to His blessing upon that daily food, in order that it may nourish and support them. For, to borrow the language of Bishop Joseph Hall,

> Indeed we live by food, but not by any virtue that is without God, without the concurrence of whose providence bread would rather choke than nourish us. Let him withdraw his hand from his creatures in their greatest abundance, we perish. Why do we therefore bend our eyes on the means, and not look up to the hand that gives the blessing? What so necessary dependence hath the blessing upon the creature, if our prayers hold them not together?[37]

Surely, we ought daily to feel and acknowledge that, without the blessing of God to make our food serve its proper end, even the very staff of life would be but a broken staff, which would have no power to help us in our time of need.

It is said in the Holy Scriptures, even of the very beasts of the earth and the fowls of the air, that they *"seek their meat from God"* (Psalm 104:21; see also Psalm 147:9). This[38] may well be termed a natural cry, or the voice of their necessity. But when Christians say, *"Give us this day our daily bread,"* this spiritual cry of prayer is the peculiar voice of God's own children. They earnestly implore God's ordinary blessing upon their daily bread. Nor do they rest here; but there is something even beyond this ordinary blessing which they chiefly desire, namely, a secret character and stamp of His peculiar favor upon all their temporal enjoyments. And this, as all God's faithful people know from their own experience, is a delightful fruit of prayer. Yes, there is a peculiar voice of God's own children in the words of this petition. And if so, we may rest assured that He distinguishes it both from the common voice of natural men and from the cry of the other creatures which call for supply, and that He returns a special answer to their prayer. Together with the daily bread, which He gives to others, and a common blessing upon it, believers have something, therefore, which is not given to others; and they feel that their daily bread and all their needful supplies are peculiarly sweetened by this one consideration, namely, that they receive them as His "gift," after a special manner, out of their Father's own hand, having humbly prayed for them.

Mindfulness of the Bodily and Spiritual Wants of Others

Moreover, while the Christian is taught in the words of this petition to look up to God as the Author and Giver of all good things, he is taught at the same time to look upon all around him as entitled to share in the benefit of his prayers. For when he utters the words *"give us this day our daily bread,"* he does, in effect, say to his heavenly Father, "Give it, not to me only, but to others in common with me." We are thus plainly reminded how necessary it is that we should cultivate a spirit of tender and compassionate concern for all the members of Christ's body; and, more especially, that, in all our prayers and even in our most secret devotions, we should ever be mindful of the bodily and spiritual wants of all around us.

The Importance of Daily Devotion

Lastly, let us observe how forcibly we learn from the very terms of the request the duty and the necessity of daily devotion. For when we are expressly commanded to ask for the food and raiment which are convenient for us only for a single *"day"*—in the words *"Give us **this day**"* (Matthew 6:11), or *"Give us **day by day** our daily bread"* (Luke 11:3)—we are assuredly bound to ask for them every day. The prayer for bread to be given *"day by day,"* or for *"this day,"* must evidently be a daily prayer. And should not this remind us that we are to renew the desire of our souls toward God as often as the wants of our bodies are renewed? Should not this remind us that, as duly as the day returns, we should pray to our heavenly Father and consider that we might as well go a day without food as a day without prayer?

Such is the full import of the petition *"Give us this day our daily bread."* And now, let us ask ourselves whether it does not exhibit the true temper and frame of a Christian mind. For, whatever may be his own lawful care and labor, and with whatever measure of success that care and labor may be attended, still that upon which the believer relies and lives is the good providence of God—not his own forethought, industry, or skill. "He lives upon that providence from one day to another as a child in his father's house. And, with regard to provision for the future, he thinks it as good in God's hand as if it were in his own."[39] If, therefore, he have much hand or great revenues, he does not trust any more in his substance than if he possessed nothing: while, under a full conviction that nothing can profit us, except as it bears the impress of the divine blessing, he knows how indispensable it is that he should day by day offer up the prayer *"Give us this day our daily bread."* And, on the other hand, if the Christian have bread for today and nothing for tomorrow—just as the children of Israel had their manna—yet he trusts no less in God than if he were possessed of thousands. In short, the believer's language always is, "Whether I have much or little, I look to my God only for the provision which I need; and it is upon His blessing in answer to prayer that I desire to live from day to day. Let *'the LORD* [be] *my shepherd'*; [and] *'I shall not want'*" (Psalm 23:1).[40]

It is plainly declared, then, in the petition which our Lord has here taught us to use, that we should approach our heavenly Father day by day as knowing ourselves to be daily dependent upon His watchful and never-failing providence, and daily to need His blessing upon all that we are or have or undertake. Let us learn, therefore, to acknowledge, with thankfulness, this dependence upon Him, who "[gives] *us day by day our daily bread*"; and let us learn also to regard this daily and hourly dependence upon "[our] *Father which is in heaven*" as a daily and hourly call upon us to consecrate all our faculties, whether of body or soul, to His service; remembering that, "*whether therefore* [we] *eat, or drink, or whatsoever* [we] *do,*" we are to "*do all to the glory of God*" (1 Corinthians 10:31). Let us learn to look to Him as the God of all grace and the Fountain of all good, both for our souls and our bodies. And may He give us a single eye and a pure heart, so that, knowing Him as a reconciled Father, we may commit our souls to Him in faith and prayer, in patience and well-doing, humbly depending on Him as His children, not only for the supply of all our bodily wants, but also for all His spiritual blessings in Christ Jesus; or, as it is expressed in our catechism, for "all things that are needful both for our souls and bodies."[41]

Spiritual Nourishment for Our Souls

This is the language used by the compilers of the catechism in paraphrasing the clause of the Lord's Prayer which is now before us. And this leads me to remark that though, in the connection in which it stands, the petition evidently relates to our temporal wants, yet, when taken in itself, it may be regarded as it was regarded by many of the early fathers[42]—in a spiritual sense, as relating also to that "*bread of God...which cometh down from heaven* [to] *giveth life unto the world*" (John 6:33); and which is as necessary to the daily nourishment and support of our souls, as the manna, which came down in the wilderness, was to the bodies of the Israelites. When pointing out the difference between the manna, which was given in the wilderness, and the living bread, which came down from heaven, Jesus says,

> *Your fathers did eat manna in the wilderness, and are dead....*[but] *if any man eat of this bread, he shall live for ever: and the bread that I will give is my flesh, which I will give for the life of the world.* (John 6:49–51)

The manna, however, was intended to foreshadow the blessings of redemption; and it may be well for us, therefore, to consider the truths which are illustrated by this remarkable type of Christ.

The manna was provided for all. And does not our Lord invite all, without exception, even all who are weary and heavy-laden, to come unto Him? The manna accompanied the people of Israel even to the borders of the Promised Land. And did not this represent, in a most affecting manner, that mystical union with Christ, by a true and lively faith, which supports the believer in all dangers and adversities, even until his life's end? And when we read how the Lord commanded Moses—that an omer full of manna should be "[laid] *up before the* L*ORD*" in the Holy of Holies *"to be kept for* [their] *generations"* (Exodus 16:33)—are we not thus forcibly reminded of the promise made by our Lord to every true believer in His message to the church of Pergamos: *"To him that overcometh will I give to eat of the* ***hidden manna****"* (Revelation 2:17)?

And blessed, indeed, would those Jews at Capernaum who listened to the words of Jesus have been had they considered what a privilege they enjoyed, beyond that of their fathers in the desert, in seeing Him whom the manna so remarkably foreshadowed. Blessed would they have been had they been prepared to receive Jesus saying *"I am the living bread which came down from heaven: if any man eat of this bread, he shall live for ever: and the bread that I will give is my flesh, which I will give for the life of the world"* (John 6:51).

But, though our Lord had told the Jews in plain terms that He was desiring to instill the necessity of faith in Himself as the promised Messiah, whom "God the Father had sealed" (see John 6:27, 29, 35); and though the image which He had been employing was evidently intended to illustrate, in a powerful and yet familiar manner, that all-important truth—still the Jews perversely disputed among themselves, saying, *"How can this man give us his flesh to eat?"* (John 6:52).

And how, indeed, could our blessed Lord have employed such language as this had He not been a greater than Moses? How indeed could our Lord have employed such language as this had He not been the High Priest of those good things to come, which the manna but faintly foreshadowed? Let all, therefore, who have hitherto regarded Jesus Christ only as a human instructor ponder in their hearts the language which our Lord employs in the sixth chapter of John; and let them say whether, on the one hand, it does not place Jesus Christ before them as the eternal Son of God, and whether, on the other hand, it does not plainly teach us that *"the life which* [we] *now live in the flesh* [we are to] *live by the faith of the Son of God, who loved* [us], *and gave himself for* [us]" (Galatians 2:20).

Jesus' Language Suggests His Sonship

Does it not place Jesus Christ before us, on the one hand, as the eternal Son of God? As we read the Scriptures, we shall often find the sacred writers representing the instructions therein contained as the food of the soul; but where shall we find it said of any other teacher that he is himself the food which we are commanded to eat? Where shall we find it said of any other teacher that we are to "eat his flesh" and "drink his blood"? Jesus says,

> *The bread of God is he which cometh down from heaven, and giveth life unto the world.* (John 6:33)

> *I am the bread of life: he that cometh to me shall never hunger; and he that believeth on me shall never thirst.* (John 6:35)

> *I am the living bread which came down from heaven: if any man eat of this bread, he shall live for ever: and the bread that I will give is my flesh, which I will give for the life of the world.* (John 6:51)

Jesus' Claim Calls for Our Faith

And if Jesus Christ is here placed before us as the eternal Son of God, are we not here taught with equal plainness that *"the life which* [we] *now live in the flesh"* we are to *"live by the faith of the Son of God, who loved* [us], *and gave himself for* [us]" (Galatians 2:20)? In other words, are we not here invited to partake, by a true and lively faith, of the benefits of Christ's mysterious sacrifice? *"Whose eateth my flesh, and drinketh my blood,"* says Jesus, *"hath eternal life; and I will raise him up at the last day"* (John 6:54). It is plain, therefore, not only that the believer has a title to eternal life, but that he has the beginning of it even here; and the resurrection of the believer's soul to a new and spiritual life is the pledge of the resurrection of his body to everlasting glory; for *"he that eateth me,"* says Jesus, *"even he shall live by me.…He that eateth of this bread shall live for ever"* (John 6:57–58). And, therefore, as we would hope to be partakers of such great salvation, we must show the reality of our faith by feeding continually on this living Bread.

Now, our Lord's injunction is express, that we should draw near to our heavenly Father day by day with the words of this petition: *"Give us this day our daily bread"*; and we have seen that if we would realize the depth and fullness of this prayer, we must remember how indispensable it is that we should ask and receive daily nourishment both for our bodies and our souls. But it is not, as we shall readily admit, the mere preparation of our natural food which nourishes and sustains the body; it must be received and wrought into the system. And, were it not for the blindness and perverseness of our hearts, we should admit with equal readiness that Jesus Christ does not give life to our souls merely by dying for us, or by being exhibited in the gospel; but only when He is received and fed upon by faith, and when we thus find our souls nourished and strengthened to every good word and work.

May we feed, then, day by day, on this living Bread, by faith, with thanksgiving! May we receive Christ by renewed exercises of penitence and faith as our daily Bread! And may we esteem it our highest privilege to receive from time to time the most comfortable sacrament of the body and blood of Christ,[43] believing assuredly that, at the holy table, the souls of believers are strengthened and refreshed by His body and blood, even as their bodies are by the bread and wine; and that they thus become *"one bread, and one body,"* since they are *"all partakers of that one bread"* (1 Corinthians 10:17). So shall we find our spirits recruited, our hearts encouraged, and our strength repaired to run the race, to endure the conflict, and to perform the work which God has appointed us until we are *"delivered from the bondage of corruption into the glorious liberty of the children of God"* (Romans 8:21)!

CHAPTER FIVE

THE PETITION FOR THE FORGIVENESS OF OUR TRESPASSES, AS WE FORGIVE THEM THAT TRESPASS AGAINST US

"And forgive us our debts, as we forgive our debtors."
—Matthew 6:12

"And forgive us our sins; for we also forgive every one that is indebted to us."
—Luke 11:4

Sufficient unto the day[44] is all that we are taught to desire in this divine prayer before us; and yet it is more than we deserve, by reason of the manifold and great transgressions, of which we have been so repeatedly guilty. Is it not evident, then, that however regular and constant may be our prayers for daily bread, we cannot reasonably expect that they will be answered unless we shall endeavor, with God's assistance, to place ourselves in such a posture before the throne of grace, as may render us meet to receive the mercies of heaven? Or, even should our daily prayer prove effectual in obtaining our daily bread, still it would profit us but little to receive and to eat that bread if we did not feel assured that we had our heavenly Father for our Friend. The children of Israel did eat angels' food and were fed with manna in the wilderness. Yet with some of them, God was not well pleased. Their sins were not forsaken and therefore not forgiven. And so it came to pass, that when God *"gave them their request;* [He] *sent leanness into their soul"* (Psalm 106:15).

God is not changed with the lapse of ages: He is *"the same yesterday, and to day, and for ever"* (Hebrews 13:8); and He will as certainly condemn and punish the evildoers now as He did the evildoers then. If, therefore, we bear within our bosoms the burden of crimes unrepented and unpardoned, it may be that, though we receive our food and raiment as a gift from heaven today, God shall visit us in His wrath tomorrow. But even should we not be visited for our iniquities in this world, and should our wants continue to be graciously supplied from day to day, still, if we carry about with us a conscience weighed down with the terrors arising from unpardoned sin, it matters little how long or in what state of life we live.[45]

True indeed it is that God makes His sun to rise both on the evil and on the good (see Matthew 4:45); but it is to the good alone that the beauty of his rising is wont to bring cheerfulness of countenance and gladness of heart. In the same manner do all the mercies of Providence fall unblessed upon the heads and hearts of the unrighteous: and to him that eats his bread in the bitterness of a spirit wounded, with the recollection of unforgiven offenses, it will neither give strength to his body nor peace to his mind.

"Forgive Us Our Debts"

From the supply, therefore, of those temporal wants, which is necessary to our existence here, our Lord immediately passes forward to the consideration of those spiritual wants, the answer to which is essential to our well-being in every state. *"Forgive us our debts* [or "trespasses"[46]]" (Matthew 6:12) is the language which Jesus enjoins to every sinner on earth; because, without the forgiveness of God, all other petitions, even if granted, will be of little avail for the purposes of inward and abiding consolation.[47]

It is upon this clause of the petition—in which we implore forgiveness of our own trespasses—that I will, in the first place, make a few remarks; under the full persuasion that, if our hearts shall be touched with a sense of our own need of mercy, and of the fullness of that mercy, which the gospel has revealed to us, we shall not need many arguments to convince us that, according to the full purport of the second clause, we ought to be merciful one to another even *"as our Father also is merciful"* (Luke 6:36).

Now the petition which we are here taught to utter is that our heavenly Father will "*forgive us our debts*" (Matthew 6:12); or, as we find it expressed in the parallel passage in Luke, that He will "forgive us our sins."[48] That the two expressions are strictly equivalent, our Lord has Himself pointed out in the solemn declaration by which, on the former occasion, the prayer was accompanied: "*For if ye forgive men their trespasses,*" says Jesus, "*your heavenly Father will also forgive you*" (Matthew 6:14). And what indeed are the sins, whether of thought, word, or deed, which we are daily and hourly committing but so many "debts" which we are daily and hourly accumulating, which we can never pay, and which need, therefore, continual remission? For do we not daily and hourly need forgiveness, not only of our former sins, but of our renewed offenses? Do we not daily and hourly need forgiveness of all our sins in thought, word, or deed; of all our sins in heart and life; of all our sins of omission and commission, in our conduct toward God and man? And do we not need to be daily and hourly reminded how little we can ever do for Him, from whom, as our Creator and Redeemer, we receive everything needful, whether for our bodies or our souls; and to whom, therefore, all should be devoted in perfect love?

In the affecting language of two of our Lord's parables, we have, in truth, "*nothing to pay*" (Luke 7:42; see also Matthew 18:23–25 and Luke 7:41–43); but, how blessed is the declaration which follows in the same parables, that when we feel and acknowledge our poverty and come before our God in the posture of poor and lowly penitents, He will frankly "forgive us all that debt"! How blessed also is the promise given by the mouth of His prophet:

> *When the poor and needy seek water, and there is none, and their tongue faileth for thirst, I the* L*ORD will hear them, I the God of Israel will not forsake them.*
>
> (Isaiah 41:17)

May it ever be deeply engraven on our hearts that here we have a pattern of prayer[49] in which Christ has taught us continually to implore the forgiveness of our sins; that as we, through the frailty of our nature, are daily subject unto sin, so we should daily exercise the acts of repentance and perpetually seek the favor of God! While we are in this life, encompassed with flesh; while the enticements of the world, the crafts of the devil, and the infirmities and corruptions of our nature betray us to the transgression of the law of God, we are always liable to offend. This, however, is the comfort of the gospel of Christ—that, while it discovers sin within us, it shows how we may be delivered from its power and its guilt; it shows us how we may apply ourselves unto God by repentance and be pardoned by His mercy and renewed by His grace.

But if we would feel still more deeply our own need of mercy for the forgiveness of our sins, we must ponder in our hearts the Scripture definition of sin as the "*transgression of the law*" (1 John 3:4), and then consider how fearful is the load of guilt which we must be daily accumulating, seeing that man's best and holiest actions are stained with imperfection and defilement. (See Isaiah 64:6.) Yes, we must consider how we ought to "acknowledge and bewail our manifold sins and wickedness, which we, from time to time, most grievously have committed, by thought, word, and deed, against [God's] Divine Majesty, provoking most justly [His] wrath and indignation against us."[50] For if the law of God be, of a truth, the rule of the actions of men, then any smallest deviation from that law is sin. Not only[51] is every thought, every word, and every deed that is in opposition to that pure and holy law to be regarded as sin, but also every evil habit contracted in the soul by the actions committed against the law of God; every corruption and inclination in the soul to do that which God forbids, or to omit that which God commands, is a sin, by which we justly provoke His wrath and indignation against us.

Great, therefore, is the need which we have to say, day by day, from the very ground of our hearts, "*Forgive us our sins.*" But, blessed be the name of Him to whom we address the prayer—"*with the Lord there is mercy, and with him there is plenteous redemption*" (Psalm 130:7). Would we know, then, the fullness of the mercy which the gospel reveals to us? Let us contemplate[52] "*God…in Christ, reconciling the world unto himself, not imputing their trespasses unto them*" (2 Corinthians 5:19). Let us contemplate the wonderful humiliation and the mysterious sufferings of the eternal Word; and let us remember that the painful and shameful death which terminated those sufferings was endured for sin. For "*this man,*" says Paul, "*offered one sacrifice for sins*" (Hebrews 10:12). Now, we are told by one apostle that "*Christ also hath once suffered for sins, the just for the unjust*" (1 Peter 3:18); and we are told by another that He was "*holy, harmless, undefiled, separate from sinners*" (Hebrews 7:26). It is plain, therefore, that the sins for which He suffered were not His own. No, it is the united testimony of the prophets and the apostles that the sins for which He suffered were not His but ours; for "*he was wounded for our transgressions*" (Isaiah 53:5), He "*was delivered for our offences*" (Romans 4:25), He "*gave himself for our sins*" (Galatians 1:4), and He "*died for our sins according to the scriptures*" (1 Corinthians 15:3). And what was this "dying for our sins"? It was suffering death as a punishment taken upon Himself to free us from the punishment due unto our sins. For God the Father has "*laid on him the iniquity of us all*" (Isaiah 53:6) and has "*made him to be sin for us, who knew no sin; that we might be made the righteousness of God in him*" (2 Corinthians 5:21). Yea, "*he hath borne our griefs, and carried our sorrows...the chastisement of our peace was upon him; and with his stripes we are healed*" (Isaiah 53:4–5); and (blessed consummation of the adorable scheme of redemption!) by suffering this punishment to free us from the penalty due unto our sins, it comes to pass that our sins are forgiven. "*For this,*" says Jesus, "*is my blood of the new testament, which is shed for many for the remission of sins*" (Matthew 26:28); and, as Paul says to the Ephesian converts, "*In* [Christ] *we have redemption through his blood, the forgiveness of sins, according to the riches of his grace*" (Ephesians 1:7).

Let us, therefore, meditate with adoring hearts on the fullness of the mercy which is revealed to us in the Scriptures of truth. For sure I am that the more we shall ponder in our hearts this glorious mystery of redemption, the more we shall admire God's goodness and the happiness of the true believer. When man was once fallen into sin, it was utterly impossible that he should be able to work out his own recovery: and yet, if it be the express declaration of God's holy and unchangeable law that the soul which sins must of necessity die, it is plain that—unless some way of escape shall be provided for the sinner, whereby that "law" may be "magnified" (see Isaiah 42:21)—the wrath of God must be abiding on him forever. But what can be imagined within the sinner which should move God not to execute His righteous sentence against him?[53] Or what can be imagined without him which could pretend to rescue him from the sentence of an almighty and offended God? Glorious, therefore, must the goodness of our God appear, who Himself takes off the guilt and who imputes not the sin. This is, indeed, the unutterable goodness of God, and this is the unspeakable happiness of the true believer; for *"blessed is he whose transgression is forgiven, whose sin is covered. Blessed is the man unto whom the LORD imputeth not iniquity"* (Psalm 32:1–2). Under the Old Testament dispensation, the year of release, the year of jubilee, was a time of public joy; but, assuredly, there is no voice like that which we hear under the gospel dispensation *"Thy sins are forgiven thee"* (Matthew 9:2, 5); for, by this, the believer is rescued from the worm that dies not; by this, he is made capable of heaven; by this, he is assured of eternal happiness.

"As We Forgive Our Debtors"

I have dwelt thus at length upon the first clause of this petition in the Lord's Prayer, because, as I have said, I am fully persuaded that if our hearts shall be touched with a deep sense of our own need of forgiveness, and of the fullness of that mercy which is revealed to us in the gospel, we shall not require many arguments to convince us that, according to the scope of the second clause, we ought to be merciful as our Father also is merciful; for, wherever Christ really dwells in the heart by faith, the reality of that faith must and will be evinced by the exercise of a love which shall embrace the whole family of man. And, accordingly, it is upon this very ground of a real, vital belief of the redemption which is in Christ Jesus that Paul beautifully enforces the exercise of

Christian forgiveness in two different epistles. "*Let all bitterness,*" says the apostle in his epistle to the Ephesians,

> *and wrath, and anger, and clamour, and evil speaking, be put away from you, with all malice: and be ye kind one to another, tenderhearted, forgiving one another, even as God for Christ's sake hath forgiven you.*
>
> (Ephesians 4:31–32)

And, in writing to the Colossians, he says still more emphatically,

> *Put on therefore, as the elect of God, holy and beloved, bowels of mercies, kindness, humbleness of mind, meekness, longsuffering; forbearing one another, and forgiving one another, if any man have a quarrel against any: even as Christ forgave you, so also do ye.*
>
> (Colossians 3:12–13)

Knowing, therefore, that, in the words of this petition, our Lord has graciously purposed to elevate our hearts and minds day by day to the true, the only standard of Christian forgiveness, the believer, as he repeats this petition, devoutly prays that, under an increasing sense of the fullness of that mercy which has been exercised toward himself, he may, indeed, be merciful as our Father also is merciful. And the earnest desires of his heart, as he gives utterance to the words which our Lord has taught us to use, may be thus expressed:

> Do thou, O Father, for Christ's sake, forgive me my debts as I forgive my debtors. Yea, let my whole life bear testimony to my thankful heart, that the gratitude, which extends not to Thee, may overflow to

> men. For how just it is, that I should show to them that mercy which I ask and want. I bless Thee for Thy goodness; I feel the constraining influence of the love of Christ; and I do now, from the bottom of my heart, naked before that presence from which no thought is hid, most freely forgive all those who, by thought, word, or deed, knowingly or ignorantly, have offended or have injured me. I lay aside all my claims to vengeance. I wish to forget all offenses that have ever been committed against me; and if I remember them at all, I desire to remember them only in my prayers, earnestly beseeching Thee, in behalf of the offenders, that Thou wouldest be pleased to change their hearts and to save their souls. And I do most ardently desire, O Father, that the sense of Thy divine and boundless love may kindle in my breast a flame of thankfulness to Thee, which no time shall quench, and may lead me to cherish an affection to men which no provocation and no wrongs shall conquer. And may this principle of heavenly love reign in my heart and direct and animate all my actions.[54]

And now let us consider how different would be the aspect of this Christian country if such were the spirit which really actuated every family and every neighborhood through the length and breadth of the land. We should then learn, it we may so express ourselves, to hate as God Himself hates; to hate, that is, not the persons of men, but their sins—not what God made them, but what they have made themselves: and we should then learn not to rest satisfied with the mere pretense and show of forgiveness. For what is it but a vain and idle pretense to talk, as so many are accustomed to talk, of forgiving, though they cannot forget the injuries which they have received? Is this the forgiveness which we desire to obtain for ourselves when we approach the throne of grace? Should we be content with such forgiveness from God; to have only a present forbearance of revenge but no further friendship, no blessed reconciliation with Him? Not such is the forgiveness which sinners need, and not such is the forgiveness which God so graciously vouchsafes to them; for, whatever may be the character of many of our reconciliations, as we call them, God's way of forgiving is to forgive and to forget; and, assuredly, if ours be not so, we have no portion in His. We know indeed that, in strictness of speech, God cannot forget the sins which have been committed against Him; and yet, what is the language in which He is pleased to convey to the penitent the blessed assurance of forgiveness? *"I will forgive their iniquity, and I will* ***remember their sin no more****"* (Jeremiah 31:34). And *"who,"* as the prophet Micah so emphatically asks,

> *is a God like unto thee, that pardoneth iniquity, and passeth by the transgression of the remnant of his heritage? He retaineth not his anger for ever, because he delighteth in mercy. He will turn again, he will have compassion upon us; he will subdue our iniquities; and* ***thou wilt cast all*** **[our]** ***sins into the depth of the sea.*** (Micah 7:18–19)

But if such be the character of the divine forgiveness, it is evident that, according to the scope of the petition before us, even such should be the character of that forgiveness which we are to exercise one toward another: and if this shall appear a hard saying, is it not because we are so apt to forget that religion has its seat in the heart and not in the head? We all know how common it is to say that they who evince an ungrateful spirit forget the kindness which has been bestowed upon them; not that such acts of kindness have really faded from their memory, but that their whole conduct betrays the utter insensibility of their cold and selfish hearts. Now, with the children of God, the reverse of all this takes place; for, while they treasure up every act of kindness in their very heart's core, they forget the injuries which they may have received. Not, indeed, that they are actually able to blot out the particular circumstances from their memory, but that the remembrance of such injuries only leads them to pray the more earnestly for the souls of those who have committed them, and that they daily and hourly endeavor with God's assistance to overcome evil with good.[55]

There are cases, indeed, as our Lord Himself has plainly shown us, in the parable of the unmerciful servant; where, owing to the perverseness of the offending party, it may not be possible to manifest this forgiveness in all its blessed extent. (See Matthew 18:16–17.) But still, the spirit of Christian forgiveness is, in every case, to be freely and fully exercised. In every case, we are to endeavor, by the exercise of patience, forbearance, and long-suffering, to gain a brother to God and to ourselves. And, whatever may be the success of our endeavors, we are still to show that we ourselves forgive the offender by forgetting the offense, as having been committed against ourselves, and by remembering it only as having been committed against God, that so our prayers may be quickened in our brother's behalf at the throne of grace.

There are many, it is to be feared, who will be absolutely startled at this portrait of Christian forgiveness. But, if so, let them ask themselves whether they have ever laid to heart the affecting truth contained in the abovementioned parable; namely, that when we are once brought to feel and acknowledge that we are *unable to pay,* our Lord "freely forgives us all that debt." If we have any sense of God's love to us, we shall never hereafter talk of our enemies. Nay, more than this, we can have no enemies, none that we shall ever consent to treat as such if we have the least glimpse of what is meant by God's love to us, or any spark of love to Him!

To fix this lesson the deeper in our hearts, let us remember, in conclusion, that even Peter, before he knew the immeasurable extent of redeeming love, could say, *"How oft shall my brother sin against me, and I forgive him? till seven times?"* Jesus answered, *"I say not unto thee, Until seven times: but, Until seventy times seven"* (Matthew 18:21–22). And, accordingly, we afterward find this same Peter thus appealing to his fellow Christians and saying, *"Be ye all of one mind, having compassion one of another, love as brethren, be pitiful, be courteous: not rendering evil for evil, or railing for railing: but contrariwise blessing"* (1 Peter 3:8–9).

May this be the spirit in which we may always dwell one with another. If ever our proud, envious, and uncharitable hearts shall rise against these heavenly precepts, may we have grace to say to our heavenly Father, from the very bottom of our hearts, *"Forgive us our debts, as we forgive our debtors"* (Matthew 6:12). And, as we pray, may we endeavor to realize to ourselves those awful words of the parable of the unforgiving servant: *"I forgave thee all that debt, because thou desiredst me: shouldest not thou also have had compassion on thy fellowservant, even as I had pity on thee?"* (Matthew 18: 32–33). For vain, and worse than vain, will be our own prayers for mercy "*if* [we] *from* [our] *hearts forgive not every one his brother their trespasses*" (Matthew 18:35).

Passages on Christian Forgiveness

> *The following passage is extracted from Bishop Jeremy Taylor's* The Whole Works of Right Rev. Jeremy Taylor, *vol. 3 [London: 1850], 470.*

"This we pray, with a tacit obligation to forgive: for so only, and upon that condition, we beg pardon to be given or continued respectively; that is, as we from our hearts forgive them that did us injury in any kind, never entertaining so much as a thought of revenge, but contrariwise loving them that did us wrong; for so we beg that God should do to us. And therefore it is but a lesser revenge to say, I will forgive, but I will never have to do with him; for if he become an object of charity, we must have to do with him, to relieve him; because he needs prayers, we must have to do with him, and pray for him: and to refuse his society when it is reasonably and innocently offered, is to deny that to him which Christians have only been taught to deny to persons excommunicate, to persons under punishment, i.e. to persons not yet forgiven: and we shall have but an evil portion if God should forgive our sins, and should not also love us, and do us grace, and bestow benefit upon us. So we must forgive others; so God forgives us."

> *The following passage is extracted from Mr. Henry Thornton's* Family Prayers: To Which Is Added a

Family Commentary on the Sermon on the Mount, *ed. Rev. Manton Eastburn (New York: Swords, Stanford, and Co., 1837), 18, 80–83.*

"And there is much need, with all of us, for watchfulness and prayer, if we would attain to this exercise of heavenly love; It is much to be suspected, that many, who freely admit the excellency of this saying of CHRIST [*"Blessed are the merciful: for they shall obtain mercy"* (Matthew 5:7)], contrive to evade it. They, for instance, who say that they freely forgive an injury but cannot forget it, break this admonition of Christ. They also, who *profess* both to forget and to forgive, may manifest by some part of their conduct that they are transgressors on this point. And even they who confer some favour on the person who has injured them, may not be clear of the sin in question; since the very pride of superiority may lead a man to confer a favour on him from whom an injury has been experienced. To receive a favour from an enemy is a better proof of a forgiving spirit than to bestow it."

…

"The forgiveness of injuries is…one of the distinguishing doctrines of Christianity.…This doctrine having been most plainly taught by CHRIST, there is no one now bearing the Christian name who refuses to give his assent to it: though, undoubtedly, there are multitudes who contrive, in one way or another, to evade it in their practice.

"We will here speak…of those occasions on which an unforgiving spirit is now apt to show itself.…

"The occasions, on which different men are apt to take offence, are indeed very different. It may however be observed, in general, that, whenever the pride of men is wounded, they are then wounded in the most tender part; and that they cannot so easily forgive an affront to their pride, as they can an injury to their interest. Let us then not fancy that we are of a forgiving spirit, because we can forgive those who have committed a trespass upon our property; because we can pardon the thief, or the house-breaker, who has robbed us, and whose injury moreover we know that the law of the land will amply revenge. Let us examine, rather, whether we forgive those who, by some act or other, have offered an affront to the natural pride of our hearts; and who, in this far more trying way, have been guilty of some 'trespass against us.' Again, it is worthy of remark, that it is by no means the greatest and most notorious injuries, which are apt to give the greatest offence. On great occasions, we know that the world observes us; and by forgiving a notable injury, we think that we shall do ourselves credit with the world. Moreover we usually find that where the injury is great, many sympathize with us, and join together in blaming the guilty persons.

"This general defamation of the man who has offended us, serves, much like the execution of the severe sentence of law, to satisfy our anger, and to quiet an unforgiving spirit. Let us not then take credit for forgiving our enemies, merely because we forgive them in cases of this sort. Let us inquire rather, whether we forgive him who injures us, when he does it in such a manner that the world takes part with him rather than with us: and when the offender seems to suffer no punishment, or inconvenience of any kind, for his offence. If we can forgive freely in cases of this kind, it is a strong mark of our having attained to a truly forgiving spirit. It is true, undoubtedly, that provocations will sometimes be given which are so very great that it is hard indeed, especially for men of certain natural tempers, not to be much ruffled by them. But it is one thing, to be agitated, and even angry, for a moment; it is another, to bear settled malice in the heart. Let us dread, above all things, to retain a secret ill-will against any one. Let us be able to say, 'There is no man on earth whom I account my enemy: I live in charity with all mankind.'

"Let us, therefore inquire, not only whether we forgive those who trespass against us; but in what sort of humour we are with them. Is it a benevolent and kind humour, an unreserved and friendly humour, a communicative and pleasant humour? Or are we reserved towards them, silent, distant, and desirous of avoiding them? Do we rejoice with them when they rejoice; and weep with them when they have any thing to make them weep; in the same manner as we did, before they trespassed against us? If the trespass be thoroughly forgiven, undoubtedly this will be very much the case: but if quite the contrary to this happen; if we feel secretly grieved at their cheerfulness and prosperity, and glad at their adversity; this is a strong mark of our not feeling towards them a forgiving spirit: for forgiveness, be it remembered, does not consist *in saying 'I forgive.'* It consists in the general temper and spirit. It consists in the perseverance of kindness after the offence. How is this as to God? We pray to be forgiven by Him, *in the same manner as we forgive others;* but when we pray for his forgiveness, do we not mean by it, that we pray for a kind and beneficent and friendly disposition in God towards us? Should we consider Him as forgiving us our trespasses, if we knew Him to be still difficult of approach, cold and distant towards us, not allowing us to draw near to Him, in prayer, as His children; but wishing us to depart from His presence, instead of inviting us towards Him?

"Let us then examine ourselves closely, respecting the nature of that forgiveness which we exercise; for in the same *manner* in which we forgive men their trespasses, our Heavenly Father will also forgive us. Oh, how great is the contrast between that forgiveness to which we lay claim, from God towards us; and our temper towards others; God, we expect, will forgive us great offences, offences many times repeated, and will forgive them freely, liberally, and from the heart. But we are offended at our neighbour, perhaps, for the merest trifles; and for an injury only once offered: and we are but half reconciled, when we seem to forgive. Even an uncertain rumour, an ambiguous word, or a suspected look will inflame our anger; and hardly any persuasion will induce us for a long time to relent: by one, offence is taken at a neglect at not answering a letter; by another, at not returning a visit; by a third, at some accidental failure in those attentions which it is chiefly the pride and littleness of our own minds that has taught us to expect. We are embittered perhaps, not against enemies, but against our very friends, by some of these causes; and we find it hard, and almost impossible, to forgive.

"How different is this treatment of others, who have trespassed against us, from that treatment which we expect at the hand of God! In order, then, to cure this temper, let us call often to mind our own trespasses against *Him*. Let us earnestly implore of Him pardon for our great offences; and while we thus pray, let us abhor the thought of retaining the slightest feeling of an unforgiving spirit towards our neighbour."

CHAPTER SIX

THE PETITION AGAINST BEING LED INTO TEMPTATION, AND FOR DELIVERANCE FROM EVIL

"And lead us not into temptation, but deliver us from evil."

—Matthew 6:13; see also Luke 11:4

Upon reviewing those clauses of the prayer which have hitherto engaged our attention, we cannot fail to remark that the several petitions of this divine prayer, which should always be regarded by us as the model of every Christian prayer and as the summary of the gospel, point out the several relations in which we stand toward God, and the various graces and dispositions which those relations imply.

In the words *"our Father which art in heaven"* (Matthew 6:9), we are reminded that we should always approach the throne of grace as the children of God, with our hearts disengaged from the things of earth, animated by the spirit of divine adoption, and desiring to be united to Him, who is the Fountain of light and life, the only Author and Giver of every good and every perfect gift.

When repeating the words *"hallowed be thy name"* (Matthew 6:9), we are reminded that we are to pray as belonging to a holy priesthood, and that our hearts, therefore, should be warmed with zeal for the glory of God, with an ardent desire for the sanctification of His name among all orders and degrees of men, and with an earnest wish so to be clothed ourselves with the garment of holiness, that we may resemble *"our Father which is in heaven"* (verse 9).

Christians are also to regard themselves as subjects desiring to proclaim the majesty of their king. We are taught, therefore, to say *"thy kingdom come"* (verse 10) and to desire that He alone may reign in our hearts; so that we may "[bring] *into captivity every thought to the obedience of Christ"* (2 Corinthians 10:5).

The true believer knows also that it is his privilege to cherish a spirit resembling that of a wife toward her husband; desiring, in all things, to obey the blessed will of the Lord God of his salvation, and seeking only to please Him. And he says, therefore, not only with his lips, but from the very ground of his heart, "*Thy will be done in earth, as it is in heaven*" (Matthew 6:10).

Moreover, when we approach the throne of grace, we should always come as sheep disposed to follow our Shepherd whithersoever He leads us, and to look to Him only for all the nourishment we require. And even such is the spirit in which we should repeat the words "*Give us this day our daily bread*" (verse 11).

Once more, we must always come to the throne of grace as penitents, imploring mercy for the forgiveness of our past transgressions, and grace to help us for the time to come; so that, under a sense of the mercy shown to us, we may "forbear one another and forgive one another" (see Colossians 3:13), "even as God for Christ's sake forgave us" (see Ephesians 4:32). Day by day, therefore, are we to offer up the words of this petition: "Forgive us our trespasses, as we forgive them that trespass against us." (See Matthew 6:12.)

Our attention has been already directed to all these several petitions; and it has been my endeavor so to illustrate their scope and signification, that we might be able to comprehend the fullness and perfection of this divine prayer, and thus be led to repeat it with the spirit of true devotion. We are now to consider the remaining petition, "*Lead us not into temptation, but deliver us from evil*" (Matthew 6:13); reserving, for the concluding section, the words of praise with which our

Lord closed the prayer when He delivered it for the first time in His Sermon on the Mount.

"Lead Us Not into Temptation"

The first clause of this petition serves to remind us that we should always approach our heavenly Father as the Great Physician of souls, acknowledging and deploring that "fault and corruption" of our nature, whereby we are "very far gone from original righteousness" and are "inclined to evil"[56]; for we are here taught daily to say, *"Lead us not into temptation"* (Matthew 6:13). And, assuredly, as we daily utter these words, we ought to feel that the way of salvation is a way of deep self-abasement, since we thus acknowledge that the grace which the gospel promises is a help which must be called into daily and active exercise by every child of God. And what, indeed, should render us more humble; what should render us more vigilant; what should lead us more frequently to the exercise of faith and prayer than the rooted persuasion that we are naturally inclined to evil, and that we have no power to do anything acceptable or well-pleasing to God except by God's grace "preventing us, that we may have a good will, and working with us, when we have that good will"?[57] What should lead us to pray more earnestly than the deep conviction that we are continually exposed to all the evil suggestions of a deceitful heart within, and to all the temptations of a wicked world without us?

The second clause of the petition, *"Deliver us from evil,"* is suited to remind us that we should always approach our heavenly Father as captive exiles, suing to Him, who only can deliver us from the bondage under which we are groaning. And when we think of all the "evils" which beset us on every side, and when we consider the warfare in which, therefore, we must necessarily be engaged, as long as we are in this world of trial, well may we plead day by day for grace to help us in time of need; and well may we long for that day of complete deliverance, when the tempter and his temptations, when all evil desires and all sinful inclinations, shall be destroyed forever![58]

Let us now proceed to consider the words of this petition somewhat more in detail; and then let us endeavor under the divine blessing to improve the subject of our meditations to our own instruction in righteousness.

Were it not that some persons have used very unwary expressions on this subject, it would be scarcely necessary to observe that, when we say, "*Lead us not into temptation,*" the words cannot imply that God is, in any sense, the author of temptation. "*Thou art not a God,*" says the psalmist, "*that hath pleasure in wickedness: neither shall evil dwell with thee*" (Psalm 5:4). "*Thy throne, O God, is for ever and ever: the sceptre of thy kingdom is a right sceptre. Thou lovest righteousness, and hatest wickedness*" (Psalm 45:6–7). "*He is the Rock,*" says Moses, "*his work is perfect: for all his ways are judgment: a God of truth and without iniquity, just and right is he*" (Deuteronomy 32:4). "*What shall we say then?*" exclaims the apostle Paul, when treating of the divine sovereignty. "*Is there unrighteousness with God? God forbid*" (Romans 9:14). And the language of the apostle James is remarkably clear and impressive: "*Let no man say when he is tempted, I am tempted of God: for God cannot be tempted with evil, neither tempteth he any man: but every man is tempted, when he is drawn away of his own lust, and enticed*" (James 1:13–14).

The last-mentioned words of the apostle, describing man as being *"tempted, when he is drawn away of his own lust, and enticed"* (James 1:14), may serve to guide us to the true interpretation of the clause *"Lead us not into temptation."* And its meaning may be expressed in the following terms: Withdraw not Thy grace from us, O Father, lest, when left to grapple[59] with our spiritual foes in our own strength, we should be *"drawn away of* [our] *own lust, and enticed."* Thou know the dangers in which we are placed. Thou know that we live in the midst of enemies who are ever plotting to destroy our souls; that we have the Prince of Darkness always going about as a *"roaring lion,...seeking whom he may devour"* (1 Peter 5:8), and the treacherous corruption of our own hearts, ready to betray us into his power; and that we have snares laid for us on every side—snares in our hours of solitude and in our hours of social intercourse; snares in our worldly occupations; snares in all the walks of public or private life; yea, snares in our most holy and spiritual exercises, even in meditation and prayer. Seeing, then, that we are thus encompassed with temptation on every side, and that we have "no power of ourselves to help ourselves,"[60] suffer us not, O Father, to be overcome by temptation, but "grant to us such strength and protection, as may support us in all dangers, and carry us through all temptations...through Jesus Christ our Lord."[61]

It is said in the tenth Article of the Church of England that we have "no power to do good works pleasant and acceptable to God, without the grace of God by Christ preventing us, that we may have a good will, and working with us, when we have that good will."[62]

Now, it will appear, from the train of thought which we have just been pursuing, that the words of this clause, *"Lead us not into temptation,"* may be considered as relating to God's "preventing grace," or the grace which should always go before us "in all our doings," so that we may always be upon the watch against all the enemies of our salvation. But we require, not only divine grace to "[prevent] us, that we may have a good will," but the same grace to assist us and "[work] with us, when we have [it]." And therefore it is that we pray to our heavenly Father, saying not only, *"Lead us not into temptation"* but also, *"Deliver us from evil"* (Matthew 6:13). In other words: Withdraw not from us Thy preventing grace, lest we be left blind and naked and defenseless amidst all the dangers and "temptations" of the world, the flesh, and the devil; and grant us, at the same time, Thy assisting grace, to "deliver us from evil." Yes, save us, we implore Thee, from evil of every kind;[63] from every evil passion and every evil thought; from every evil word and every evil work; from every evil being and every evil thing; from the wickedness of man, the malice of the devil, and the danger and deceitfulness of our own corrupted nature. Yea, may Thy grace be continually "working with us," that so we may be saved "from all sin and wickedness, and from our spiritual enemy, and from everlasting death."[64]

Now, when we think of all these "evils," from which we pray that we may be delivered, we might well shrink from venturing, in our own strength, upon such a fearful conflict. "Alas!" might the Christian say, when looking upon the temptations without and the corruptions within himself; and, when considering how slow has been the growth of that measure of grace which he has already received, "Alas! how shall this be? How shall I ever attain my journey's end?" But, when the

Christian looks upward; when he lifts his eyes above his difficulties and beholds the strength of God engaged in his behalf; when he directs his prayer to Him for help and is assured that he shall find it—this upholds him and dissipates all his fears. For what though there be a *"roaring lion"* (1 Peter 5:8) that seeks to devour us? Still also there is "a strong rescuing lion,"[65] even *"the Lion of the tribe of Judah"* (Revelation 5:5), who will deliver all believers from this cruel adversary. *"Yes,"* says the apostle Paul, *"the God of peace shall bruise Satan under your feet shortly"* (Romans 16:20). He says not, be it observed, "We shall bruise Satan under our feet," but *"God"* shall do it. Yet it is not said that God shall bruise him under His own feet but under ours; that is, as all believers gather joyfully from these words, the victory shall be theirs, though wrought by God. We should observe, moreover, that the apostle here speaks of God as the *"God of* ***peace.****"* For it is as if he had said to all the children of God, "Because He is the God of peace, be assured that He will finally subdue that great disturber of your peace, and will admit you into those courts of the heavenly temple, where the Wicked One ceases from troubling, and where the weary shall enter into endless peace."

Instruction in Righteousness

Having thus considered the scope and signification of the words *"Lead us not into temptation, but deliver us from evil"* (Matthew 6:13), we are now to endeavor, with God's assistance, to improve the subject of our meditations to our instruction in righteousness. And, to this end, I would offer two remarks; the one arising out of the connection of this petition with that immediately preceding; the other, out of the words themselves, as showing the necessity of watchfulness and prayer.

The Connection in Matthew 6:12–13

Let us, then, first consider the connection of the petition before us with the petition immediately preceding.[66] In that petition, we pray to our heavenly Father, beseeching Him "to forgive us our trespasses, as we forgive them that trespass against us" (see Matthew 6:12); and when, therefore, we say immediately afterward, *"Lead us not into temptation, but deliver us from evil"* (verse 13), do we not plainly gather from the connection of these two petitions that we need to be rescued from the dominion, as well as to be freed from the damnation, of sin? In other words, do we not gather from the connection of the two petitions that, while we need the blood of Christ to purchase for us forgiveness of sins, and so to deliver us from the guilt and condemnation of sin, we need the Spirit of Christ to rescue us from its power?

I observed in the last section that the man who feels most deeply his own need of mercy to cover his past transgressions will be the first to exercise forgiveness toward others, and to be merciful even as his Father also is merciful. And I may now add that the same deep and abiding sense of his need of divine mercy to cover all his past sins will ever be accompanied by such an experimental acquaintance with the power of indwelling sin and the treachery of his own heart, as must lead the believer to pour out many a fervent prayer for grace, to carry him through all temptations and to deliver him from all evil.

The Necessity of Watchfulness and Prayer

We have thus seen from considering the petition before us in connection with the petition immediately preceding how it is suited to remind us that we must pray day by day to be delivered from the power, as well as from the guilt and condemnation, of sin; and if we now dwell, in conclusion, on the particular scope of the petition itself, we shall see how it is suited to inculcate the necessity of watchfulness and prayer.

Watchfulness

"Watch and pray," says Jesus, *"that ye enter not into temptation"* (Matthew 26:41); and, accordingly, as often as we repeat the petition *"Lead us not into temptation, but deliver us from evil,"* we should be reminded, on the one hand, of the necessity of watchfulness. Indeed,[67] if there be truth in the observation which I have already made, namely, that snares surround us on every side—in our solitude and in our social converse; in our more public or in our more private duties; and even in our most holy and spiritual employments—yea, if it be true that when we would do good, evil is present with us, surely there cannot be a minute of our lives in which we can be exempted from the duty of Christian watchfulness. Day by day and hour by hour, we must be "[putting] *off concerning the former conversation the old man, which is corrupt according to the deceitful lusts"* (Ephesians 4:22); and more than that, we must day by day and hour by hour be "[putting] *on the new man, which after God is created in righteousness and true holiness"* (Ephesians 4:24). For, not only are we *"not"* to be *"conformed to this world,"* but, as Paul exhorts the Roman converts, we must be *"transformed by the renewing of* [our] *mind"* (Romans 12:2). And, if we attend to the exact force of this latter clause of the exhortation, we

should have little difficulty understanding what the apostle means when he warns us in the preceding clause "not to be conformed to this world"; for it is evident that only they who are *"not conformed to this world"* are continually *"transforming"* themselves *"by the renewing of* [their] *mind."*

We are, therefore, deluding our own souls if we imagine that Paul is here calling upon us to abandon the station of life to which it has pleased God to call us, or to neglect, in any the smallest degree, the duties and the relations of social life. We may shut ourselves out from the busy haunts of men, and we may choose to hold intercourse only with those who will adopt the same narrow and exclusive notions with ourselves; but, however secluded may be our daily walk, and however narrow may be the circle of our acquaintance, still the world will follow us everywhere and entwine itself with all the inmost affections of our hearts, unless those hearts shall be transformed by the renewing influence of the Holy Spirit.

It follows, therefore, that they only understand the apostle's precept who have learned, by divine grace, not to shut themselves out from the world, but to shut out the world with all its sinful practices from their own hearts and minds; and that they only are the true soldiers of the cross who, instead of deserting the post in which they have been stationed by the Captain of their salvation, are endeavoring, with His assistance, to overcome all the dangers and temptations of this sinful world by a daily and hourly transformation of their hearts and minds. With this view, they resolve to *"take unto* [them] *the whole armour of God"* (Ephesians 6:13); and, in the expressive language of one of our old writers, they never think of laying aside their armor until others shall be called upon to wrap them in their shroud.

Prayer

But, while the command to watch is to call forth our activity in all the ways of a holy obedience, the command to pray is to remind us that we have no power of ourselves to help ourselves, but that all our strength is placed in another. In vain, then, shall we resolve to watch and strive against all the onsets of the world, the flesh, and the devil, unless, by the exercise of earnest and fervent prayer, we shall engage the Holy One of Israel to place underneath us His everlasting arms, that, in His strength, we may indeed be strong. For we are plainly reminded in Scripture that *"except the LORD build the house, they labour in vain that build it"*; and that *"except the LORD keep the city, the watchman waketh but in vain"* (Psalm 127:1): and, therefore, while we watch and labor as if the work were to be all our own, we must believe and pray as if it were all God's.

To revert, then, to the language of the petition before us, as, on the one hand, we hope not to be "led into temptation," we must pray to our heavenly Father for that preventing grace which shall open our eyes to see the dangers to which we are exposed from the world, the flesh, and the devil. As, on the other hand, we hope to be "delivered from evil," we must pray for that assisting grace, which, by rescuing us now "from all sin and wickedness," may be regarded as a pledge and an earnest of our final deliverance hereafter from "our spiritual enemy, and from everlasting death."[68]

May we watch, therefore, and pray that we enter not into temptation. Yea, may we be

> *...strong in the Lord, and in the power of his might. [Putting] on the whole armour of God, that [we] may be able to stand against the wiles of the devil....Praying always with all prayer and supplication in the Spirit, and watching thereunto with all perseverance.*
>
> (Ephesians 6:10–11, 18)

And then we may rest assured that the *"God of peace will bruise Satan under* [our] *feet shortly"* (Romans 16:20), and that He will finally *"deliver us from* [all] *evil"* (Matthew 6:13) through Jesus Christ our Lord.

Excerpt from Dr. Isaac Barrow on "Lead Us Not into Temptation"

"The word [*temptation*] is commonly taken in a worse sense, for an occasion presented with ill purpose, or naturally tending and not easily avoided, of falling into sin; a stumbling-block, a snare; as when St. Paul saith, that *they who will be rich, do fall εἰς πειρασμὸν καὶ παγίδα, into temptation and a snare* [1 Timothy 6:9]; thus St. James assureth us that *God tempteth no man* [James 1:13]; that is, doth not intend to seduce or inveigle any man into sin. Yet because nothing in the world, either good or bad, doth happen without God's permission and governance; and the Devil himself must obtain license from God, before he can tempt any man, or do any mischief (as we see in Job's case, and in the history of Ahab;) since God seeth whatever is done, and with greatest ease could hinder it; and doth not otherwise than for some good end suffer any evil to be designed or achieved; it is the style of Scripture to attribute such things in some sense to him; as when God is said to *send Joseph into Egypt to preserve life*

[Genesis 45:5]; whenas in truth his brethren, out of envy and ill-will, did sell him thither; and, God is said to *move David to number the people* [2 Samuel 24:1]; whenas indeed Satan (as it is otherwise affirmed) *provoked him to number them* [1 Chronicles 21:1]: and that horrid tragedy acted by the Jews upon our blessed Saviour is said to be brought to pass by the *hand and definite counsel of God* [Acts 2:23; 4:28]; because God, foreseeing the temptations which those men should incur of committing such acts, and their inclinations to perform them, did resolve not to interpose his power in hindrance of them, but suffering them to proceed, would turn their mischievous practices to an excellently good end, and use them as instruments of his just, holy, and gracious purposes: thus then, whereas by *temptation* here is meant any occasion alluring or provoking to sin, or withdrawing from duty, with a violence, all things considered, exceeding our strength to resist or avoid...God may be said to bring them into it, whom in justice he permits to be exposed thereto; although he do no otherwise intermeddle, or concur therein, than by not affording, or by withdrawing, his especial direction and assistance; leaving them without check blindly or wilfully to follow the sway of their own tempers, the instinct of their vain minds, the bent of their corrupt wills, the violence of their unruly passions and appetites; letting them to fall into the manifold snares of false opinion, evil custom, and contagious example, which the world sets before them...permitting the devil, without control or impediment, by his wiles to delude and seduce them; which kind of proceeding of God with men is clearly represented in the 81st Psalm; where, of the Israelites, God says, that having signally declared his pleasure to them, and by promise of great benefits invited them to observe it, upon their wilful neglect, he dealt thus with them: *But,* says God there, *my people would not hearken to my voice, and Israel would none of me; so I gave them up unto their own hearts' lusts; and they walked in their own counsels* [Psalm 81:11–12]. In such manner, if God, provoked thereto by our heinous miscarriages, doth justly bring us into, or doth let us *enter into temptation* (as our Lord otherwhere expresseth it; *Pray,* saith he, *that ye enter not into temptation* [Luke 22:40, 46]), we shall infallibly run into many grievous sins and desperate mischiefs; no less surely, than we shall wander and stumble in the dark, than we shall slide and fall in the most slippery places, and sometimes be entangled, when we do walk in the midst of snares, surrounded with traps innumerable, most cunningly laid to catch us: *It is not* (saith the prophet) *in man to direct his steps* [Jeremiah 10:23], so as to go straight and upright; it is not in him to see his duty, to bend his inclinations to compliance therewith; to restrain his appetites, when sensible objects forcibly press on them; to govern his passions, when they are vehemently stirred to disorderly motion; we do continually need God's instruction to guide us, God's *hand to uphold us* [Psalm 37:24], God's care and help to guard us: when therefore, I say, our condition and circumstances do minister dangerous occasions of sin; when our vain and weak tempers do incline or betray us thereto; when the world would smile or frown us into it [for the world by its fair promises and pleasing flatteries enticeth to sin or, by its angry frowns and fierce threats, discourageth from goodness]; when the Devil violently solicits, or thrust on toward it; thus to be destitute of God's grace, thus to be left to ourselves, is the most horrible judgment that can be. In such cases and seasons, God's interposal is necessary, either to remove those temptations, or to support and defend us from the prevalence of them, *φυλάσσων ἀπταίστους, keeping us from stumbling and falling* [Jude 24], as St. Jude speaks; *not suffering us,* as St. Paul expresseth it, *to be tempted above what we are able, but making with the temptation also a way to escape, so that we shall be able to sustain it* [1 Corinthians 10:13]."[69]

CHAPTER SEVEN

THE DOXOLOGY, OR THE THANKFUL ACKNOWLEDGMENT OF GOD'S ETERNAL AND EVERLASTING KINGDOM, POWER, AND GLORY

"For thine is the kingdom, and the power, and the glory, for ever. Amen."
—Matthew 6:13

The words of this doxology, or form of praise, are found only in the gospel according to Matthew. It is, in substance, the same with a doxology which was in use in the Jewish church; and we may conclude, therefore, that our Lord saw fit to adopt it from the Jewish liturgy. But, as we do not find it in the gospel by Luke, we must infer that, when our Lord delivered this divine form of prayer on the second occasion, He omitted the words of the doxology. We find, indeed, that, in the Latin copies of the New Testament, it is omitted even in the gospel by Matthew; but, as the clause is found in the Syriac version, which can be traced up to the earliest ages of the Christian church; as it is introduced into the Greek liturgies (as it is utterly improbable that the holy fathers of the Greek church should presume to add their own inventions to a form which our Lord had Himself delivered to His disciples); and as it is difficult to understand why the clause, if added afterward, should not have been introduced into the gospel by Luke as well as the gospel by Matthew, we may safely receive this doxology as part of the Lord's Prayer. It is, moreover, so perfectly scriptural in its character, and so full of profitable instruction, that the internal evidence of its divine origin seems to be quite unanswerable.

It was, as we may suppose, upon these grounds that the venerable compilers of our own liturgy deemed it right to preserve the clause, not only when the prayer is introduced for the first time at morning and at evening prayer, but in certain other parts of *The Book of Common Prayer*, when the occasion seems more especially to call for praise and thanksgiving;[70] while, in the remaining parts of the liturgy, we are taught to repeat this divine prayer as it is found in Luke, without this doxology.

Not that the omission of this particular clause is to be regarded as an omission of praise; seeing that the whole prayer, independent of the doxology, is, in truth, one beautiful and comprehensive form of adoration to the praise and glory of the Most High. For is not the praise of our heavenly Father set forth by us in this prayer when we call upon Him as *"our Father which art in heaven"* (Matthew 6:9), beseeching Him, that His "name may be hallowed" (see verse 9); that His *"kingdom* [may] *come"* (verse 10); that His *"will* [may] *be done in earth, as it is in heaven"* (see verse 10); when we put up these petitions to Him alone; and when we refer everything to His will and His glory? Every clause of this prayer, therefore, is virtually in praise of God: and it is, perhaps, exactly that species of praise which, on almost all occasions, is most fit to be used by strangers and pilgrims like ourselves, who must feel that their praises should always be mingled with fervent prayers for mercy and for grace. For, assuredly, the pure, unmixed language of praise must be reserved for that state when they who have "[come] *out of great tribulation"* (Revelation 7:14) shall join the ranks of the church triumphant and shall unite in singing praise to Him who *"sitteth upon the throne, and unto the Lamb"* (Revelation 7:10). And blessed, indeed, are they who, after a daily repetition of this prayer on earth, shall, hereafter, be permitted to exchange their hosannas for hallelujahs and say, "Hallowed be Thy name, O Lord; for thy kingdom is come, Thy will has been accomplished. Our sins are forgiven; the season of trial and temptation has passed away, and we have been delivered from all evil. Thine, indeed, is the kingdom; and to Thee be ascribed all power and glory forever and ever. Amen."[71]

The Doxology of God's Kingdom, Power, and Glory

Let us now consider the words of this doxology as they stand in connection with the several petitions which have already passed under our review; and, that we may give them the largest interpretation which, in this connection, they may seem to admit, let us view them in three different lights: namely, as constituting a special form of praise and thanksgiving, pointing out the fit accompaniment of prayer; as constituting the reasons upon which the preceding petitions are grounded; and as pointing out the end and purpose to which all our devotions should be directed.

A Special Form of Praise and Thanksgiving

In the first place, we will consider these words as constituting a special form of praise and thanksgiving and denoting the fit accompaniment of prayer. Viewing them in this light, they may serve to remind us that the thankful acknowledgment of former mercies and deliverances, and of the divine attributes and perfections, will always be found to be a great help and encouragement in our addresses at the throne of grace; in other words, we must have *praising hearts* before we can ever hope to approach the throne of grace with such *praying hearts,* as may find acceptance with "*our Father which* [is] *in heaven.*" Do we, then, really believe and joyfully acknowledge that His is the "*kingdom,*" or "dominion"; that His is the "*power*" and His is the "*glory, for ever*" (Matthew 6:13)? If so, this belief and this acknowledgment will be a strong encouragement to us to pray that His kingdom may come in full strength and power. Do we often ponder in our hearts, and thankfully acknowledge, the proofs which He has given of both His almighty power and of His readiness to "stretch forth the right hand of [His] Majesty, to be our defence against all our Enemies"?[72] If so, this consideration will operate as a strong encouragement to us to pour out our hearts before Him in fervent and persevering prayer.

"I was cast upon thee from the womb" (Psalm 22:10), says David; and, having experienced the divine care and protection all his life long, he feels encouraged to say, *"Be not far from me; for trouble is near; for there is none to help* [me]*"* (verse 11).

The Reasons upon Which the Other Constitutions Are Grounded

In the next place, this leads me to consider the words of this doxology as constituting an enforcement of the preceding petitions; that is, as being the reasons upon which those petitions are grounded. We beseech our heavenly Father to grant the things which we have prayed for; and why? Even because "[His] *is the kingdom, and the power, and the glory*" (Matthew 6:13). The words are thus connected with the preceding petitions as forming the very ground upon which we venture to offer them up to God, and upon which we trust that He will be pleased to grant them. And it is, therefore, as if we should say,

> If we desire, O Lord God, that "Thy name may be hallowed" (see Matthew 6:9); that *"thy kingdom* [may] *come"*; and that *"thy will* [may] *be done in earth, as it is in heaven,"* it is because *"thine is the kingdom, and the*

power, and the glory, for ever" (Matthew 6:13). Seeing, therefore, that You are so great and glorious a King, and that Your dominion endures throughout all generations, may we not come with holy confidence to pray that all good things may be bestowed upon us and that all evil may be averted from us; that we may find You gracious to us both in giving and forgiving; and that, as You do forgive us the guilt of our sin, so You will vouchsafe to free us from its power? We are under Your almighty protection; we are Your subjects, yea, Your children; for You are our King and our Father: and sure[73] we are that, to whatever sum our debts amount, they cannot rise above the height of Your goodness, which rises far above the highest thought of men or angels. Sure we are, likewise, that, be the multitude of our enemies what it may, we need not fear, since all their force cannot be above Your scepter; and *"thine is the kingdom."* Our enemies, it is true, may be strong, too strong for us; yet, in Your sight, they are *"as nothing,"* yea, *"less than nothing"* (Isaiah 40:17), for all power is Thine. And this we know, moreover, that all the good which You give upon us will bring back glory to Your name, for Thine, also, is the *"glory, for ever"*!

We pray to You, therefore, that Thy name may be hallowed, because You are the *"KING OF KINGS, AND LORD OF LORDS"* (Revelation 19:16); and because the exercise of Your power for this end will tend to Your glory. We pray to You, that Thy kingdom may come; or, in other words, that Your throne may be established in the hearts of men; because to You only it appertains to rule in men's hearts; because You only can bless the means which are to be employed for the advancement of this kingdom of grace; and because, in so doing, *"thine* [will be] *the glory, for ever"*!

We pray that *"thy will be done in earth, as it is in heaven,"* because the inhabitants of the earth, as well as the angels in heaven, are Your subjects and owe You obedience; because this is a part of Your universal kingdom, though too long revolted from You; because the power is in Your hand to recover us from our enmity against You, by affording both the outward means and the inward grace; and because this will tend both to our happiness and to Your honor and glory.

We ask You to *"give us this day our daily bread"* (Matthew 6:11), because You *"watereth the hills from* [Your] *chambers:* [and] *the earth is satisfied with the fruit of thy works"* (Psalm 104:13); because You bring forth *"grass to grow for the cattle, and herb for the service of man"* (verse 14); and because it is for Your honor and glory that all should *"wait...upon thee; that thou mayest give them their meat in due season"* (verse 27).

We ask You to "forgive us our trespasses, as we forgive them that trespass against us" (see Matthew 6:12), because You have established a kingdom in which *"mercy and truth are met together"* (Psalm 85:10); because You have invited all that are weary and heavy laden to come unto Thee (see Matthew 11:28); and because, as You declare Your "Allmighty power, most chiefly in shewing mercy, and pity,"[74] so we believe that You will be chiefly glorified in the exercise of that mercy through Your Son, our Savior, Jesus Christ.

Lastly, we ask You to *"lead us not into temptation, but deliver us from evil"* (Matthew 6:13), because we know that our *"adversary the devil, as a roaring lion, walketh about, seeking whom he may devour"* (1 Peter 5:8); because we know that he is seeking either to withdraw us altogether from Your service or to corrupt us in our obedience to You, our rightful Lord and King; and because we know that we cannot hope to withstand his crafts and assaults unless we take refuge under the wings of Your almighty power, and unless we continually beseech You to glorify Yourself in the salvation of our souls: *"for thine* [only] *is the kingdom, and the power, and the glory, for ever"* (Matthew 6:13)!

Where All Our Devotions Should Be Directed

Thus, in the third place, we are led to consider the words of this doxology as pointing out to us the one end and purpose to which all our devotions should be directed; namely, the honor and glory of God. This, indeed, is the line[75] under which all our prayers ought to move. All our petitions should be regulated by it; and they may certainly be regarded as irregular when they swerve and wander from it. We may observe, also, from carefully examining this divine prayer that the line here marked out for our devotions is a circular line; the exercise of prayer being, as Archbishop Leighton so beautifully observes, "like that of the heavens, a circular motion."[76] For the prayer before us begins and ends at the same point; namely, the glory of God, to whom we pray, and who is the God that hears and answers prayer. In that point, the Lord's Prayer begins, and in that point, it ends; and if the requests which regard ourselves are placed in the middle, we are hereby plainly taught that all our desires should move in this heavenly circle. Yes, we are here distinctly reminded (and I pray that the lesson which is thus inculcated may be deeply engraven on our hearts!) that, though the things for which we pray, whether temporal or spiritual, concern ourselves, yet they are not to terminate in ourselves but in Him who is the First and the Last, the Beginning and the End of all things! For we are to desire, not only the blessings of this life, but the blessedness of the life to come more for His glory than for our own good.

Viewing the words of the doxology under this last aspect, we plainly learn that, as often as we approach the throne of grace, God's glory should be the one grand scope and mark toward which we should direct all our petitions; so that we should desire the things for which we pray, not only as being good for ourselves, but as being suited to help us in the service of our God. And, assuredly, if we thus viewed the words of this doxology, we should learn to pray as those who desire "perfectly [to] love [God], and worthily to magnify [His] holy Name."[77] We should learn never to rest in any inferior good but, in all our petitions, to aim at a higher and a nobler purpose. In praying, for instance, for a blessing on the means which we may employ, we should never forget the end for which we are to employ them. And, in praying to the Author and Giver of every good and perfect gift for any valuable talent, we should be always careful to pray, at the same time, for grace, to employ it in His service and for His glory!

Instruction in Righteousness

Having thus briefly considered the words of the doxology as reminding us how praise should accompany prayer, as constituting the reasons upon which the preceding petitions are grounded, and as pointing out the aim and end to which all our devotions should be directed, let us now endeavor, under the divine blessing, to bring the words home to our hearts, for our own guidance and instruction in our Christian pilgrimage.

God's Kingdom: The Whole World Is Under His Government

If, then, the *"kingdom"* be God's, let us rest our souls upon this comfortable truth; namely, that the whole world is under His government. If He who is the King of all the earth be, indeed, our *"refuge and strength,"* then surely we need not fear, *"though the earth be removed, and though the mountains be carried into the midst of the sea;* [no,] *though the waters thereof roar and be troubled,* [and] *though the mountains shake with the swelling thereof"* (Psalm 46:1–3). If God governs the world, then it shall, and it must, be well with all them who fear God. They may safely resign themselves to Him and disburden all their anxieties in His bosom. And they may rest well assured of this, that all things shall indeed work together for good to them that love Him. (See Romans 8:28.) Not but that there are many dark and difficult things in God's providence which cannot be fathomed by our weak and limited understandings; but the language of the believer is, "Though I walk in darkness, and have no light; yet I will trust in the name of the Lord, and stay upon my God." (See Isaiah 50:10.) And, while the believer thus learns to have honorable conceptions of God and His kingdom, he learns, also, to live in entire and cheerful obedience to His laws; to have no intercourse with any of His enemies; and to be "*faithful*" to Him even "*unto death,*" so that he may obtain a "*crown of life*" (Revelation 2:10). Is God indeed the King of all the earth? Then, in the midst of all the trials and difficulties to which we may be exposed; amidst all the temptations of the world around us and all the suggestions of our own sinful hearts within us, let us commit our way to Him in fervent, humble, believing prayer, and He will bring it to pass!

God's Power: No Weapon Against His Kingdom Shall Prosper

If, again, the "*power*" be God's, let us stay ourselves upon this blessed persuasion, that no force or fraud of the devil or man shall be able to wrest the scepter out of His hand or to do us any the smallest injury but by His permission, for His own wise ends and purposes. If God's authority be over all, and if His power be equal to His authority, assuredly no weapon formed against His kingdom shall prosper.

> *The floods have lifted up, O Lord, the floods have lifted up their voice; the floods lift up their waves. The Lord on high is mightier than the noise of many waters, yea, than the mighty waves of the sea.* (Psalm 93:3–4)

God's Glory: The Glory of All Good Things Is God's

Once more, if, in all things, the "*glory*" be God's, then does it follow that the glory of all the good things for which we are commanded to pray is God's likewise? And is not this a source of real and abiding consolation—namely, that our duty and our happiness do not draw one way and God's glory another, but that one and the same method answers both these ends, or, rather, that these are one and the same thing; so that we cannot better set forth God's honor than by setting forward the salvation of our souls? Let this, then, be our comfort—that our holiness and happiness and the glory of God are always moving in the same blessed circle. And let this truth also be deeply impressed on our hearts; namely, that the honor of all the good that we do is due to God alone. For it is He that "direct[s], sanctif[ies], and govern[s] both our hearts and bodies, in the ways of [His] laws, and in the works of [His] commandments"[78]; it is He that gives us the means for the accomplishment of all good things; and it is He that supplies us with grace to use those means aright; so that, in all things, the glory of all is due unto Him!

There yet remains to be noticed one circumstance, which crowns all the rest; namely, that the kingdom of which we pray to be subjects, the power to which we would flee for refuge amidst all the strife and tumult of this unquiet world, and the glory of which we hope to partake are forever![79] We read of one who, when, amidst all the pomp and grandeur of a stately triumph in ancient history, was asked by one of his own courtiers, "What was wanting there?" immediately he returned for answer that "*continuance* was wanting." And where, indeed, shall we look for any earthly glory of which it can be said that it ever continues in one stay? The golden-headed image in Nebuchadnezzar's vision had brittle feet; and hence it was that it fell to pieces and became like the chaff of the summer thrashing-floor. (See Daniel 2:34–35.) Nay, more than this, not only do things on earth decay, but the very heavens themselves shall wax old like a garment. (See Psalm 102:26.) *"But thou art the same, and thy years shall have no end"* (Psalm 102:27). Here, then, is a kingdom which can never be shaken; here is a power that can never be controlled; here is a glory that can never fade; and, therefore, here is a lasting motive for our preferring these our petitions to our heavenly Father under the full persuasion that, if we are earnest in our supplications, He will always fulfill them, as He shall see to be "most expedient for [us]; granting us in this world knowledge of His truth, and, in the world to come, life everlasting."[80]

It is under this blessed persuasion that the believer adds, from the very bottom of his heart, "Amen." Verily, O Father, so would I have it; this is my wish. And verily so do You let it be; this is my prayer. When we repeat the word *amen*, which is so significant in the original, as to be left untranslated in our Authorized Version, we yield our cordial assent to all that has gone before; thus following up our petitions with winged desires and with hearty affections, proceeding from the warmth of true devotion and earnestly pressing what has been already uttered in the prayer. And it is even more than this, for it is a signification of our faith and hope to obtain that for which we have prayed.

Oh! may this, then, be the spirit, even the spirit of Christian faith and Christian hope, in which our prayers may always be offered; and then shall our petitions rise upon these two wings to the throne of the Eternal! Yes, may we always be prepared in faith and in hope to add our hearty "Amen" to this and every other prayer which we offer up to *"our Father which art in heaven"* (Matthew 6:9). And, not resting here, let the whole complexion of our lives return a cordial "Amen" to the prayers of our lips. Let us endeavor day by day to ratify the prayers which we utter by hallowing, in all our life and conversation, the name of *"our Father which art in heaven"*; by obeying the laws of His kingdom; and by doing His will on earth, as it is in heaven! And then we may rest assured that He will *"give us day by day our daily bread"* (Luke 11:3); that He will "forgive us our trespasses," seeing that "we forgive them that trespass against us" (see Matthew 6:12); and that He will "not suffer us to fall into temptation, but will deliver us from evil" (see verse 13); because "[His] *is the kingdom, and the power, and the glory, for ever. Amen"* (verse 13)!

APPENDIX A

BISHOP JEREMY TAYLOR'S PARAPHRASE OF THE LORD'S PRAYER[81]

Our Father

Merciful and gracious, Thou gavest us being, raising us from nothing, to be an excellent creation, efforming us after Thy own image, tenderly feeding us, and conducting and strengthening us all our days: Thou art our Father by a more excellent mercy, adopting us in a new birth, to become partakers of the inheritance of Jesus: Thou hast given us the portion and the food of sons; O make us to do the duty of sons, that we may never lose our title to so glorious an inheritance.

Let this excellent name and title, by which Thou hast vouchsafed to relate to us, be our glory and our confidence, our defence and guard, our ornament and strength, our dignity, and the endearment of obedience, the principle, of a holy fear to Thee our Father, and of love to Thee and to our brethren, partakers of the same hope and dignity.

Unite every member of the Church to Thee in holy bands; let there be no more names of division, nor titles and ensigns of error and partiality; let not us who are brethren contend, but in giving honour to each other, and glory to Thee, contending earnestly for the faith, but not to the breach of charity, nor the denying each other's hope. But grant that we may all join in the promotion the honour of Thee our Father, in celebrating the Name, and spreading the family, and propagating the laws and institutions, the promises and dignities of our elder Brother; that despising the transitory entertainments of this world, we may labour for and long after the inheritance to which Thou hast given us title, by adopting us into the dignity of sons. For ever let Thy Spirit witness to our spirit, that we are Thy children; enable us to cry, Abba, Father.

Which Art in Heaven

Heaven is Thy throne, the earth Thy footstool. From Thy throne Thou beholdest all the dwellers upon earth, and triest out the hearts of men, and nothing is hid from Thy sight. And as Thy knowledge is infinite, so is Thy power uncircumscribed...and Thou sittest in Thy own essential happiness and tranquillity, immovable and eternal. That is our country, and thither Thy servants are travelling; there is our Father, and that is our inheritance; there our hearts are, for there our treasure is laid up till the day of recompence.

Hallowed Be Thy Name

Thy Name, O God, is glorious, and in Thy Name is our hope and confidence. According to Thy Name, so is Thy praise unto the world's end. They that love Thy Name shall be joyful in Thee; for Thy Name which Thou madest to be proclaimed unto Thy people is, "The Lord, the Lord God, merciful and gracious, long-suffering, and abundant in goodness and truth, keeping mercy for thousands, forgiving iniquity, and transgression, and sin, and that will by no means clear the guilty." In this glorious Name we worship Thee, O Lord; and all they that know Thy Name will put their trust in Thee. The desire of our soul is to Thy Name, and to the remembrance of Thee. Thou art worthy, O Lord, of honour, and praise, and glory, for ever and ever: we confess Thy glories, we rejoice in Thy mercies, we hope in Thy Name, and Thy saints like it well; for Thy Name is praised unto the end of the world; it is believed by faith, relied upon by a holy hope, and loved by a great charity. All Thy Church celebrates Thee with praises, and offers to Thy Name the sacrifice of prayers and thanksgiving.

Thou, O God, didst frame our nature by Thy own image, and now Thou hast imprinted Thy Name upon us; we are Thy servants, the relatives and domestics of Thy family, and Thou hast honoured us with the gracious appellative of Christians. O let us never dishonour so excellent a title, nor by unworthy usages profane Thy holy Name, but for ever glorify it. Let our life be answerable to our dignity; that our body may be chaste, our thoughts clean, our words gracious, our manners holy, and our life useful and innocent; that men, seeing our good works, may glorify Thee our Father which art in Heaven.

Thy Kingdom Come

Thou reignest in Heaven and earth: O do Thou rule also in our hearts; advance the interest of religion; let Thy Gospel be placed in all the regions of the earth, and let all nations come and worship Thee, laying their proud wills at Thy feet, submitting their understandings to the guidance of Jesus, conforming their affections to Thy holy laws. Let Thy kingdom be set up gloriously over us, and do Thou reign in our spirits by Thy Spirit of grace; subdue every lust and inordinate appetite, trample upon our pride, mortify all rebellion within us, and let all Thine and our enemies be brought into captivity, that sin may never reign in our mortal bodies; but that Christ may reign in our understanding by faith, in the will by charity, in the passions by mortification, in all the members by a right and a chaste use of them. And when Thy kingdom that is within us hath flourished, and is advanced to that height whither Thou hast designed it, grant Thy kingdom of glory may speedily succeed; and that we Thy servants be admitted to the peace and purity, the holiness and glories, of that state where Thou reignest alone, and art all in all.

Thy Will Be Done in Earth, as It Is in Heaven

Thy will, O God, is the measure of holiness and peace; Thy providence the great disposer of all things, tying all events together, in order to Thy glory and the good of Thy servants, by a wonderful mysterious chain of wisdom. Let

Thy will also be the measure of our desires: for we know that whatsoever Thou sayest is true, and whatsoever Thou doest is good. Grant we may submit our wills to Thine, being patient of evils which Thou inflictest, lovers of the good which Thou commandest, haters of all evil which Thou forbiddest, pleased with all the accidents Thou sendest; that though our nature is weaker than Angels', yet our obedience may be as humble, our conformity to Thy will may arise up to the degrees of unity, and theirs cannot be more; that as they in Heaven, so we on earth may obey Thy will promptly, cheerfully, zealously, and with all our faculties: and grant that as they there, so all the world here, may serve Thee with peace and concord, purity and love unfeigned, with one heart and one voice glorifying Thee our heavenly Father.

Grant that we may quit all our own affections, and suspect our reasonings, and go out of ourselves, and all our own confidences; that Thou being to us all things, disposing all events, and guiding all our actions, and directing our intentions, and overruling all things in us and about us, we may be servants of Thy Divine will for ever.

Give Us This Day Our Daily Bread

Thou, O God, which takest care of our souls, do not despise our bodies which Thou hast made and sanctified, and designed to be glorious. But now that we are exposed to hunger and thirst, nakedness and weariness, want and inconvenience, give unto us neither poverty nor riches, but feed us with food convenient for us, and clothe us with fitting provisions, according to that state and condition wherein Thou hast placed Thy servants: that we may not be tempted with want, nor made contemptible by beggary, nor wanton or proud by riches, nor in love with any thing in this world; but that we may use it as strangers and pilgrims, as the relief of our needs, the support of our infirmities, and the oil of our lamps; feeding us till we are quite spent in Thy service. Lord, take from Thy servants sad carefulness and all distrust, and give us only such a proportion of temporal things as may enable us with comfort to do our duty.[82]

Forgive Us Our Trespasses, as We Forgive Them That Trespass Against Us

O dear God, unless Thou art pleased to pardon us, in vain it is that we should live here; and what good will our life do us? O look upon us with much mercy, for we have sinned grievously against Thee. Pardon the adherent imperfections of our life, the weakness of our duty, the carelessness of our spirit, our affected ignorance, our indiligence, our rashness and want of observation, our malice and presumptions. Turn Thine eyes from our impurities, and behold the brightness and purest innocence of the Holy Jesus; and under His cover we plead our cause, not that Thou shouldest judge our sins, but give us pardon, and blot out all our iniquities; that we may never enter into the horrible regions where there are torments without ceasing, a prison without ransom, reproaches without comfort, anguish without patience, darkness without light, a worm that never dies, and the fire that never goeth out.

But be pleased also to give us great charity, that we may truly forgive all that trouble or injure us, that by this character Thou mayest discern us to be Thy sons and servants, disciples of the Holy Jesus; lest our prayer be turned into sin, and Thy grace be recalled, and Thou enter into a final anger against Thy servants.

Lead Us Not into Temptation

Gracious Father, we are weak and ignorant, our affections betray us, and make us willing to die; our adversary, the devil, goeth up and down, seeking whom he may devour; he is busy and crafty, malicious and powerful, watchful and envious; and we tempt ourselves, running out to mischief, delighting in the approaches of sins, and love to have necessities put upon us, that sin may be unavoidable. Pity us in the midst of these disorders, and give us spiritual strength, holy resolutions, a watchful spirit, the whole armour of God, and Thy protection, the guard of Angels, and the conduct of Thy Holy Spirit, to be our security in the day of danger. Give us Thy grace to fly from all occasions to sin, that we may never tempt ourselves, nor delight to be tempted; and let Thy blessed providence so order the accidents of our lives, that we may not dwell near an enemy; and when Thou shalt try us, and suffer us to enter into combat, let us always be on Thy side, and fight valiantly, resist the devil, and endure patiently, and persevere constantly unto the end, that Thou mayest crown Thine own work in us.

But Deliver Us from Evil

From sin and shame, from the malice and fraud of the devil, and from the falseness and greediness of men, from all Thy wrath, and from all our impurities, good Lord, deliver Thy servants.

Do not reserve any thing of Thy wrath in store for us; but let our sins be pardoned so fully, that Thou mayest not punish our inventions. And yet if Thou wilt not be entreated, but that it be necessary that we suffer, Thy will be done; smite us here with a father's rod, that Thou mayest spare us hereafter: let the sad accidents of our life be for good to us, not for evil; for our amendment, not to exasperate or weary us, not to harden or confound us: and what evil soever it be that shall happen, let us not sin against Thee. For ever deliver us from that evil, and for ever deliver us from the power of the evil one, the great enemy of mankind; and never let our portion be in that region of darkness, in that everlasting burning, which Thou hast prepared for the devil and his angels for ever.

For Thine Is the Kingdom, the Power, and the Glory, For Ever and Ever. Amen

So shall we Thy servants advance the mightiness of Thy kingdom, the power of Thy majesty, and the glory of Thy mercy, from generation to generation for ever. Amen.

APPENDIX B

DR. SAMUEL OGDEN'S PARAPHRASE OF THE LORD'S PRAYER[83]

Our Father, Which Art in Heaven, Hallowed Be Thy Name

Abba, Father! Thou author, preserver, support of my being, life, hopes, and happiness; who hast brought me into this world, Thy work; and redeemed me by Thy only-begotten Son through Thy Holy Spirit to an eternal inheritance in heaven—I acknowledge Thy authority and Thy affection with reverence and gratitude. I own Thy paternal power and tenderness, and approach Thy presence with the sentiments of a son—with fear and love and joy. Thus emboldened, I raise my thoughts from earth to heaven; I look up to that seat where Thou hast dwelt from eternity, enthroned in majesty above all height, and clothed with light which no eye can bear to behold. But, though Thy glory is unsearchable, and I cannot see Thee as Thou art, yet so much, at least, I can discern of Thee by Thy image, expressed in Thy Word and reflected from Thy works, that Thou art great and just and holy. Thou wilt be *"sanctified in them that come nigh* [Thee]" (Leviticus 10:3). Thou requirest truth in the hearts of Thy worshippers; and that the lips which presume to utter Thy hallowed name be free both from impurity and fraud. May the number be multiplied, without measure, of such as present this *"incense...unto* [Thy] *name, and a pure offering"* (Malachi 1:11). And, oh, that my voice also might be heard among those who thus adore Thee!

Thy Kingdom Come

But, alas! We have been enemies to our God, rebels to Thy rightful sway; we have followed the dictates of pride and passion, have been seduced by the tempter, led astray by our own corrupt mind, or by the wiles of others; and Thy world hath lain under the power of the Evil One. How long, O Lord, holy and true? Thy time will surely come (let it come speedily!) when Thy just dominion shall be universally acknowledged in every region by every heart; when Thou shalt reign unrivalled in all Thy works; and the usurped authority of that false spirit, which divides and deforms Thy kingdom, shall be utterly destroyed forever.

Thy Will Be Done in Earth as It Is in Heaven

In heaven, Thy will is the only law. *"Thousand thousands* [minister] *unto* [Thee], *and ten thousand times ten thousand* [stand] *before* [Thee]" (Daniel 7:10) who cease not day and night to celebrate and to serve Thee with uninterrupted praises and unerring obedience. Oh, that such fidelity were found on earth! Oh, that the sons of men did even now resemble that blest society, to which they hope hereafter to be united! Oh, that they were animated with the like holy, ardent zeal, and could give themselves to God with the same entire devotion! We are blind and vain, but Thou art wise and good. Wise, therefore, in Thy wisdom, secure under Thy care, great and happy in humility and subjection, we have no wishes but in Thee. Our whole desire and glory is to be, to do, and to suffer whatever Thou art pleased to appoint.

Give Us This Day Our Daily Bread

During our passage through this perishable state, we trust and know that Thou, who gavest us life, wilt give us also all such things as are necessary for its support; and we ask no more. But oh! leave us not destitute of that *"bread…which cometh down from heaven"* (John 6:33). Let our souls be nourished by Thy Word and ordinances, that we may grow in grace and be made partakers of a life which will never end. We ask not for wealth or fame or power, but we ask for grace to *"lay up for* [ourselves] *treasures in heaven, where neither moth nor rust doth corrupt, and where thieves do not break through nor steal"* (Matthew 6:20). The one object of our desires is the light of

Thy countenance; even the approbation and the applause of our God!

Forgive Us Our Trespasses, as We Forgive Them That Trespass Against Us

But what have I said? Ah, me! Can I hope to be justified when I am judged? Dare I trust to that fiery trial? Will my life, or will my heart, endure the inspection of Thy pure eye? No; but (blessed be Thy holy name!), there is forgiveness; there is mercy with Thee. "Have mercy upon [me], most merciful Father; for thy Son our Lord Jesus Christ's sake, forgive [me] all that is past."[84] Then shall my life bear testimony to my thankful heart; and that gratitude, which extends not to Thee, shall overflow on men. For how just is it that I should show to them that mercy which I ask and want! I bless Thee for Thy goodness, and I feel the constraint of love; and I do now, from the bottom of my heart, naked before that presence, from which no thought is hid, most freely forgive all those who, by word or deed, knowingly or ignorantly have offended or have injured me. I lay aside all my claims to vengeance. I wish to forget all offenses that have ever been committed against me; and if I remember them at all, I desire only to remember them in my prayers, earnestly beseeching Thee in behalf of the offenders, that Thou wouldst be pleased to change their hearts and save their souls. And I do most ardently desire, O Father, that the sense of Thy divine and boundless love may kindle in my breast a flame of thankfulness to Thee, which no time shall quench; and may lead me to cherish an affection to men which no provocation, no wrongs, shall conquer. And may this principle of heavenly love reign in my heart and direct and animate all my actions!

Lead Us Not into Temptation, but Deliver Us from Evil

I am willing, moreover, that it should be called forth and cultivated by exercise and discipline. And, whatever trials or sufferings Thy wisdom sees fit for this happy end, I cheerfully embrace them all. Show me no hurtful indulgence. I decline no danger for Thy glory, for the good of men, for the improvement of my own soul. Yet remember that I am but dust. Be Thou near me in those perilous moments. Let not the storms of trouble and trial overwhelm me. Strengthen my failing faith. When I sink, stretch forth Thy hand. I rely on Thy providence and grace, that Thou wilt deliver me from the danger or support me under it. Save me from sin, from the great enemy of souls, and from eternal misery!

These, Lord, are the requests which my heart pours out unto Thee. But Thou seest the wants which it doth not know; Thou hearest the desires which it cannot utter. Give us what is good, though we ask it not; and mercifully deny when we pray for evil.

For Thine Is the Kingdom, and the Power, and the Glory, For Ever and Ever. Amen

My soul falls down with the lowest reverence before Thy throne, adding its little homage to the devout adoration of all Thy servants upon earth, and to the triumphant hallelujahs of the whole company of heaven; saying, "Power and honor, dominion and glory, infinite and everlasting, be unto Thee, my Lord, my Father, and my God! Amen! Amen!"

ENDNOTES

1. "A Catechism," *The Book of Common Prayer* (1928), Justus.anglican.org, http://justus.anglican.org/resources/bcp/1928/Catechism.htm.
2. Martin Luther somewhere speaks of the creeds as the science of sciences; of the commandments as the law of laws; and of the Lord's Prayer as the prayer of prayers; that is, he regarded them all as models in their several classes.
3. See the passage quoted at length in volume 4 of the Help to Knowledge series, 46–47.
4. The author of a volume of poems called *The Cathedral* has given different metrical paraphrases of the Lord's Prayer, expressive of what may be supposed to be the mind of the devout worshipper, as he utters this divine prayer in the different services and offices of the Church of England.
5. "Seeing that we have an Advocate with the Father for our sins, when we who have sinned conic to seek for pardon, let us allege unto God the words which our Advocate hath taught. For since His promise is our plain warrant, that, in His name, what we ask we shall receive, must we not needs much the rather obtain that for which we sue, if not only His name do countenance but also His

very speech present our request?"—Saint Cyprian
6. Richard Hooker, *The Words of That Learned and Judicious Divine, Richard Hooker, in Eight Books of the Laws of Ecclesiastical Polity* (London: 1723), 164.
7. See Dean Comber on the liturgy.
8. Collect for the Seventh Sunday After Trinity, *The Book of Common Prayer* (1786, 1789, 1892, 1928), http://justus.anglican.org/resources/bcp/1789/Readings1789&1892C.htm.
9. "As for the appellation *Father*, it doth mind us of our relation to God, who, upon many grounds and in divers high respects, is our Father; (by nature, for that he gave us our being, and made us after his own image; by providence, for that he continually preserveth and maintaineth us; by grace, for that he renewed us to his image in righteousness and holiness; by adoption, for that he alloweth us the benefit and privilege of his children, assigning an eternal inheritance to us)" (Isaac Barrow, *The Theological Works of Isaac Barrow*, ed. Rev. Alexander Napier, vol. 7 [Cambridge: The University Press, 1859], 407). "It is natural for children in any danger, strait, or want, to fly to their parents for shelter, relief, and succour: and it is so likewise for us to have recourse unto God, in all those cases, wherein no visible means of help appear from elsewhere: and to do so the title of Father doth encourage us, signifying not only power and authority over us, but affection and dearness toward us: the name God, importing his excellent perfections; the name Lord, minding us of his power and empire over us, with the like titles declarative of his supereminent majesty, might deter us, being conscious of our meanness and unworthiness, from approaching to him; but the word Father is attractive and emboldening; thinking on that we shall be apt to conceive hope, that, how mean, how unworthy soever, yet being his children, he will not reject or refuse us; for, *'If men, being evil, do give good gifts unto their children; how much more will our Father, which is in heaven, give good things to them that ask him?'*" (Ibid., 408.)
10. Collect for All Saints' Day, *The Book of Common Prayer*, http://justus.anglican.org/resources/bio/62.html.
11. "For ourselves, necessity compelleth us to pray, 'My Father.'
For our brethren, charity inviteth us to pray, 'Our Father.'
In these words, 'Our' and 'Father,' the law and prophets are comprehended.
In 'Father,' the love of God.
In 'Our,' the love of our neighbor.
And in these two words the sum of the Gospel is contained. In 'Father' faith. 'Our' charity"
(*Institutions Pice*, ed. Archdeacon Hale).
12. See Rev. Joseph Benson's sermon on Luke 11:2 and Archbishop Robert Leighton's on the Lord's Prayer.
13. "Our prayers are directed to our Father in heaven; because, though He hears them wheresoever they are uttered, yet He nowhere hears them with acceptance save only in heaven.

"And the reason is, because our prayers are acceptable, only as they are presented before the Father through the intercession of the Son. Now the Son performs His mediatorial office only in heaven; for He performs it in both natures, as He is not only God but Man, sitting at the right hand of the Father. And, therefore, we are still concerned to pray to our Father which is in heaven. God, indeed, hears us upon earth; for there is not a word in our tongue, *"but, lo, O LORD, thou knowest it altogether"* (Psalm 139:4). But this will not avail us unless God hears our prayers a second time, as repeated over in the intercession of Jesus Christ and perfumed with the incense which He offers up with the prayers of all the saints." (See Ezekiel Hopkins, *The Works of Ezekiel Hopkins, D.D., Successfully Bishop of Raphoe and Derry,* vol. 1 [Philadelphia: Leighton Publications, 1863], 65.)

"They also too are in heaven," says Saint Cyril, "who bear the image of the heavenly, in whom God is *dwelling* and walking in them." (See Saint Cyril, *The Catechetical Lectures of S. Cyril, Archbishop of Jerusalem* [Oxford: 1839], 276.)

14. Archbishop Robert Leighton.

15. "Let Thy Name, Thy essence, and Thy glorious attributes be honored and adored in all the world, believed by faith, loved by charity, celebrated with praises, thanked with the Eucharist; and let Thy name be hallowed in us as it is in itself." (See Bishop Jeremy Taylor, *Bishop Jeremy Taylor's Life of Our Lord and Saviour, Jesus Christ,* ed. Robert Philip [London: 1836], 275.)

"We say, *'Hallowed be thy name,'* not that we wish for God that He may be hallowed by our prayers, but that we ask of Him that His name may be hallowed in us....We ask and pray that we, who have been sanctified in baptism, may persevere therein, wherein we have begun to be." (See Saint Cyprian quoted in Saint Augustine of Hippo, *Treatise on Rebuke and Grace* [Aeterna Press].)

16. "By a rare complication, this sentence doth involve both praise and petition; doth express both our acknowledgment of what is and our desire of what should be. We do, I say, hereby partly acknowledge and praise the supereminent perfections of God above all things, in all kind of excellency, joining in that seraphical doxology (which to utter is the continual employment of the blessed spirits above), and confessing with the heavenly host that the *'Holy, holy, holy, LORD God Almighty'* (Revelation 4:8) is worthy *"to receive glory and honour and power'* (verse 11). We do also partly declare our hearty wishes, that God may be everywhere held in highest veneration; that all things relating to Him may receive their due regard; that all honor and praise, all duty and service, may in a peculiar manner be rendered unto Him by all men, by all creatures, by ourselves especially; that all minds may entertain good and worthy opinions of Him; all tongues speak well of Him, celebrate and bless Him; all creatures yield adoration to His name and obedience to His will; that He be worshipped in truth and sincerity, with zeal and fervency. This, particularly in the prophet Isaiah and by Saint Peter, is called "sanctifying God's name" (see Isaiah 29:23),

in opposition to idolatrous and profane religion. (*'Sanctify the* L*ORD* *of hosts himself; and let him be your fear, and let him be your dread'* [Isaiah 8:13], saith the prophet; and *'Be not afraid of their fear, neither be troubled; but sanctify the Lord God in your hearts'* [1 Peter 1:14–15], saith the apostle.) Thus do we here pray and wish in respect to all men and to all creatures capable of thus sanctifying God's name; but, more particularly, we pray for ourselves, that God would grant to us that we, by our religious and righteous conversation, may bring honor to His name; so that *'men* [who] *see* [our] *good works,* [may] *glorify* [our] *Father which is in heaven'* (Matthew 5:16; see also 1 Peter 2:12). 'Vouchsafe, O Father, that we may live so purely that all men by us may glorify Thee': so descants Saint Chrysostom." (See Isaac Barrow, *The Works of the Learned Isaac Barrow,* vol. 1 [London: 1716], 487.)

17. "A Prayer for the Conditions of All Men," *The Book of Common Prayer* (1928), http://justus.anglican.org/resources/bcp/1928/MP.htm.

18. Ibid.

19. For the substance of these remarks, I am indebted to John Miller's Bampton Lectures (1817).

20. "The Articles of Religion of the Methodist Church," umc.org, http://www.umc.org/what-we-believe/the-articles-of-religion-of-the-methodist-church.

21. "The Order for the Burial of the Dead," *The U.S. Book of Common Prayer* (1798), http://justus.anglican.org/resources/bcp/1789Selections/Burial.htm.

22. Ibid.; see Revelation 6:10–11.

23. "...the kingdom of grace being in order to the kingdom of glory, this, as it is principally to be desired, so may possibly be intended chiefly: which, also, is the more probable, because the address of this prayer being to God the Father, it is proper to observe that the kingdom of grace, or of the Gospel, is called the kingdom of the Son; and that of glory, in the style of the Scripture, is the kingdom of the Father" (Jeremy Taylor, *The Whole Works of Right Rev. Jeremy Taylor,* vol. 3 [London: 1839], 74).

24. Robert Leighton, *The Works of Robert Leighton, D.D., Archbishop of Glasgow* (Edinburgh: Thomas Nelson, 1844), 461.

25. "The feeling of zeal for God's glory so pervaded the heart of Jesus Himself, and He knew it to be one of so absorbing a character in all God's children, that not only has He placed the expression of it foremost in the prayer, but He has supplied, for that expression, notwithstanding the exceeding brevity of the whole composition, not less than three separate sentences, or, rather, a threefold outlet for the inward rush of feeling. For, in the feebleness of language, and its utter inadequacy to express the more intense emotions, this is the only expedient to which men can have recourse—to piece out, as it were, the scantiness of the material employed—to make up for the insufficiency of one form of utterance, by the addition of another, and another, which together may supply the symbol, if not the perfect picture, of our inward mind, and indicate the length and breadth of those emotions to which we would fain give

full expression—*'Hallowed be thy name,'* exclaims the Christian to his Heavenly Father; *'Thy kingdom come, thy will be done in earth, as it is in heaven.'*" —Griffith on the Lord's Prayer

26. "These three petitions are addressed to God by way of adoration. In the first (*'Hallowed be thy name'*), the soul puts on the affections of a child and divests itself of its own interest, offering itself up wholly to the designs and glorifications of God. In the second (*'Thy kingdom come'*), it puts on the relation and duty of a subject to her legitimate prince, seeking the promotion of his regal interest. In the third (*'Thy will be done in earth, as it is in heaven'*), she puts on the affections of a spouse, loving the same love, and choosing the same object, and delighting in unions and conformities." (See Jeremy Taylor, *The Whole Works of the Right Rev. Jeremy Taylor, D.D.*, vol. 2 [London: 1850], 468.)

"And in the three following petitions (*'For thine is the kingdom, the power, and the glory, for ever'* [Matthew 6:13]), which concern ourselves, the soul hath affections proper to her own needs, as in the former proportion, to God's glory. In the first of them, she expresses the affection of a poor, indigent, and necessitous beggar; in the second, of an offending but penitent servant; in the last, of a person in affliction or danger. And, after all this, the reason of our confidence is derived from God." (See Ibid.)

27. John Keble, "The Annunciation of the Blessed Virgin Mary," 1827.

28. See Lancelot Andrewes, *Ninety-six Sermons*, trans. John Posthumus Parkinson, vol. 5 (Oxford: J. H. Parker, 1843), 400, 402–403.

29. "God's will must be done *by* us; and then we may cheerfully consent that it should be done *upon* us, for He can will no evil to those that serve Him." —Dean Comber

"One portion of God's will is done *toward* us, to exercise our patience and our faith; and one is done *by* us, to exercise our obedience and our activity." —Augustus Hare

"'The best man in the field today,' said a general, 'was a soldier who had his arm lifted up against an enemy, but who, on nearing the trumpet sound a retreat, checked himself and dropped his arm without striking a blow.'" —Augustus Hare

30. Compare Psalm 40 with Hebrews 10.

31. Saint Augustine.

32. "The first petition that the natural man makes is for his daily bread; but our care must be, first, for the kingdom of God; next, for the fulfilling of God's will, and doing that righteousness which God requires at our hands; and, afterward, we may, in the third place, pray for such things as we stand in need of during our life. This order the fathers observe in the blessing which Isaac pronounced upon his sons. Jacob's blessing was, first, *"the dew of heaven,"* and then, *"the fatness of the earth,"* showing that the godly do prefer heavenly comforts before earthly. Esau's blessing was, first, *"the fatness of the earth,"* and next, *"the dew of heaven"* (Genesis 27:28), to teach us that profane persons do make more

reckoning of earthly commodities than of heavenly comforts." (See Lancelot Andrewes, *Ninety-six Sermons*, 414–415.)

33. We are directed to ask, says John Chrysostom, for *τροφήν, ού τρυφήν*, for necessary food, not for luxurious plenty or delicacy.

34. "To save us from losing ourselves in a wood of cares and anxieties, Christ warns us to keep out of the wood, and to be content with the shelter of a single tree." —Augustus Hare

35. The original Greek word used in this verse for "*bread*" is *ἐπιούσιον*, which denotes what is sufficient for our present support and subsistence, in opposition to *περιούσιον*, denoting what is abundant or superfluous.

36. "'Give us this day our daily bread': that is, whenever the future becomes darkened, may I no longer think thereon but simply clasp Thy guiding hand!" —Griffith on the Lord's Prayer

"In this clause of the Lord's Prayer, we declare the sense we have of our total dependence upon God; avowing ourselves to subsist by His care and bounty and disclaiming, consequently, all confidence in any other means to maintain and support us; in any store we have laid up, or estate we pretend to; in any contrivance or industry we can use; in any succor of friends or relations; for that, notwithstanding all these, we do need our daily bread to be dealt to us by God, and must continually beg it as a gift from His hands. We should not, therefore, desire to be set out of God's house or His immediate protection and care. This in itself cannot be (for God cannot alienate His goods from Himself, nor can we subsist out of His hand); nor must we desire that it should be. It is a part of atheism or infidelity of heathenish profaneness and folly to desire it. '*These things*,' saith our Lord, '*do the Gentiles seek*' (Matthew 6:32). That is, they are covetous of wealth and careful for provisions to live without dependence upon God. But we must esteem God's providence our surest estate, God's bounty our best treasure, God's fatherly care our most certain and most comfortable support; '*casting all* [our] *care upon him*,' as being assured that '*he careth for* [us]' (1 Peter 5:7); that '[He] *will never leave* [us], *nor forsake* [us]' (Hebrews 13:5); and that He will not withhold what is necessary for our comfortable sustenance." (See Isaac Barrow, *The Works of Dr. Isaac Barrow*, vol. 7 (London: 1831), 13–14.)

37. Joseph Hall, *The Works of the Right Reverend Joseph Hall*, vol. 2 (Oxford: University Press, 1863), 345.

38. See Archbishop Robert Leighton's writing on the Lord's Prayer.

39. See Robert Leighton, *The Whole Works of the Most Reverend Father in God, Robert Leighton, D.D., Archbishop of Glasgow*, vol. 4 (London: 1825), 86.

40. I subjoin a passage from one of Bishop Reginald Heber's parish sermons, beautifully illustrating the full scope and signification of this clause of the Lord's Prayer.

"When we witness the many dangers which threaten the springing of the rising corn; when we reckon up in our thoughts the opposite dangers of drought or of moisture, of parching heat, or of pinching and untimely cold; the blights, which may taint the ear; the worm, which may consume the root; and all the other alarms which the husbandman feels or fears; we cannot but perceive that something more than the industry of man is required to make him happy or prosperous; and that it is, with good reason, that, in our daily prayers, we ask our daily bread of God: since no day in the year can be found in which His blessing is not needed either to preserve the seed or to prosper the tender stalk; or to fill the ear; or to rebuke the mildew, or the storm, by which the maturer crop is endangered. And, even when the food of many days is waving before our eyes, we cannot choose but feel an anxious joy, a solemn, and, in some degree, a mournful thankfulness, when we compare our own unworthy lives with the unbounded mercies of God; when we recollect how little and how seldom we have thought on Him, who careth for us continually; and when we tremble, lest, even now, our sins should interrupt the stream of His mercy, and that the improper use, which we too often make of plenty, should, even yet, turn our abundance into hunger." (See Reginald Heber, *Sermons on the Lessons, the Gospel, or the Epistle, for Every Sunday in the Year*, vol. 2 [London: 1837], 66–67.)

41. "A Catechism," *The Book of Common Prayer* (1928), http://justus.anglican.org/resources/bcp/1928/Catechism.htm.

42. "Christ is the Bread of Life, and this Bread belongs not to all men, but to us; and as we say, "Our Father," because the Father of the understanding and believing, so we speak of "Our Bread," because Christ is the Bread of us who appertain to His body." —Saint Cyprian

43. The custom of daily communion in the early church is sufficiently proved by the following remarkable passage from Saint Cyprian: "We pray that this Bread be given us day by day, lest we who are in Christ and who daily receive the Eucharist for food of salvation, should, by the admission of any grievous crime, and our being therefore shut out from communion and forbidden the heavenly food, be separated from the body of Christ." (See Saint Cyprian, *Saint Cyprian on the Lord's Prayer* [London: 1904], 47.)

44. See Joseph Benson's sermon on Matthew 6:11–13.

45. "After the supply of food, pardon for sin is asked for, in order that he who is fed by God may live in God; and that provision be made not only for the present and temporal life, but also for the eternal, whereunto we may come if our sins are pardoned,—sins which the Lord calls OUR DEBTS, as He says in His Gospel, *I forgave thee all thy debt because thou desiredst Me*" (Saint Cyprian, *Saint Cyprian on the Lord's Prayer*, 51–52).

"After taking his food, what would encumber the soldier on his march? A heavy weight to carry. Therefore, the petition *'Give us this day our daily bread'* (Matthew 6:11) is aptly followed by the clause 'Forgive us our trespasses' (see verse 12), because, unless we are pardoned, we can neither fight nor march to good purpose." (See Augustus William Hare, *The Alton*

Sermons [London: 1874], 456–457.)
46. "Trespasses" comes from the Tyndale Bible translation (1526).
47. "Now having already desired at God's hands the glory of God's Kingdom, the good of grace for the doing of His will, and all outward good things necessary for this life, we are of necessity to pray that God will forgive us our sins, which otherwise will hinder us of these good things; and as our sins do hinder God's graces that they cannot come to us, so they hinder our prayers that they cannot come to God, for our sins are as it were 'a cloud' to hide God, so that 'our prayers cannot pass through'" (Lancelot Andrews, *Ninety-six Sermons*, 425).
48. In old English, i.e., in Anglo-Saxon and Norman, the word for "guilt," or "trespass, and "debt," or "fine," is all one: *gylt*, guilt or debt: *forfait*, trespass or fine. Perhaps, therefore, the word *opeianuata* has the same twofold meaning. —Editor
49. See Bishop John Pearson's Article X, "The Forgiveness of Sins," in his book *Exposition of the Creed* (1659).
50. "The Order for the Administration of the Lord's Supper or Holy Communion," *The Book of Common Prayer* (1928), http://justus.anglican.org/resources/bcp/1928/HC.htm.
51. See Bishop Pearson's Article X.
52. Ibid.
53. Ibid.
54. A paraphrase of Dr. Samuel Ogden's prayer in Samuel Ogden and Thomas Smart Hughes, *Sermons* (London: 1832), 73.
55. See note at the end of this section.
56. Article 9 of Religion, *The Book of Common Prayer* (1789, 1892, 1928), http://justus.anglican.org/resources/bcp/1928/Articles.htm.
57. Article 10 of Religion, *The Book of Common Prayer* (1789, 1892, 1928), http://justus.anglican.org/resources/bcp/1928/Articles.htm.
58. "When we say, '*Deliver us from evil*,' then are we reminded that we have not yet attained the region of that blessedness where no evil shall be suffered anymore. And this last thought, with which the Lord's Prayer is summed up, is so comprehensive, so sufficient for every state of trouble, that, be the Christian in what trial he may, this *final deliverance* forms the ultimate object of his groanings. The longing for this brings out his warmest tears; with aspirations toward this, he begins his supplication; on the hope of this, he lingers through their course; and, with his whole soul fixed on this, he brings them to a close." —Saint Augustine
59. "*And lead us not into temptation, O Lord.* Does then the Lord teach us to pray thus,...that we may not be tempted at all? And how is it said elsewhere, 'the man who is not tempted, is unproved;' and again, *My brethren, count it all joy when ye fall into divers temptations* [James 1:2]; or rather does not the entering into temptation mean the being whelmed under the temptation? For

the temptation is like a winter-torrent difficult to cross. Some then, being most skilful swimmers, pass over, not being whelmed beneath temptations, nor swept down by them at all; while others who are not such, entering into them sink in them....Listen...to the company of unscathed saints, giving thanks for deliverance from temptation, *For Thou, O God, hast proved us; Thou hast tried us like as silver is tried. Thou broughtest us into the net; Thou laidest affliction upon our loins. Thou hast caused men to ride over our heads; we went through fire and through water; but Thou broughtest us out into a wealthy place* [Psalm 66:10–12]. Thou seest them speaking boldly, because they passed through and were not pierced. *But Thou broughtest us out into a wealthy place;* now their coming into a wealthy place, is their being delivered from temptation" (Saint Cyril, *The Catechetical Lectures of S. Cyril, Archbishop of Jerusalem*, 277–278).

60. Collect for the Second Sunday in Lent, *The Book of Common Prayer* (1689), http://justus.anglican.org/resources/bcp/1689/Readings_1689.htm.

61. Collect for the Fourth Sunday After the Epiphany, *The Book of Common Prayer* (1689), http://justus.anglican.org/resources/bcp/1689/Readings_1689.htm.

62. Article 10 of Religion, *The Book of Common Prayer* (1789, 1892, 1928), http://justus.anglican.org/resources/bcp/1928/Articles.htm.

63. "As for such evils as these; the want of things necessary or convenient for us; bodily disease and pain; disappointment in our designs, and ill success in our undertakings; disgrace and reproach upon our good names; dangers, difficulties, and distresses concerning our outward estate; distractions, vexations, and troubles of mind about temporal matters, with the like evils (in some sense, in some degree evils, or appearing such to our natural sense and fancy;) we may indeed deprecate them (as even our Lord himself did), with submission (as he did) to the wisdom and will of God, in case it pleaseth him, and he thinketh fit to remove them: but all these things being but names and empty sounds in comparison to spiritual and eternal evils (such as are vicious distempers of mind; indispositions to serve God; ill progress in our spiritual affairs; dissatisfaction concerning our state in respect to God; actual transgression of God's holy will and law; incurring God's displeasure and disfavour; being deprived of his grace and assistance; wanting the communion and comfort of his Holy Spirit; remorse of conscience, and anguish of spirit, for having violated or neglected our duty; blindness of mind, hardness of heart; want of love, reverence, devotion toward God, of charity and good-will toward our neighbour; of sobriety, humility, regularity of passion, and calmness of temper, in respect to ourselves and the inward frame of our souls; these, I say, and such like evils), we should absolutely request of God, that he in mercy would deliver and free us from them; they being irreconcilably repugnant to his will and glory, and inconsistent with our eternal welfare"(Isaac Barrow, *The Works of Isaac Barrow, D.D.*, vol. 3 [New York: 1845], 11–12).

"If *Lead us not into temptation* had implied the not being tempted at all, He

would not have said, *But deliver us from the evil.* Now the evil is the Wicked Spirit who is our adversary, from whom we pray to be delivered" (Saint Cyril, *The Catechetical Lectures of S. Cyril, Archbishop of Jerusalem*, 278).
"The man of the world looks to himself and calls those things 'evil' which are displeasing to himself. The Christian looks to God and calls those things 'evil' which are displeasing to Him." —Augustus Hare
64. "A Catechism," *The Book of Common Prayer of the Church of Ireland: Catechism and Confirmation*, http://justus.anglican.org/resources/bcp/Ireland/Ireland_Catechism&Confirmation.htm.
65. Archbishop Robert Leighton, *The Works of Robert Leighton, D.D., Archbishop of Glasgow*, vol. 3 (London: 1805), 296.
66. "As God lets go His hold so must we let go ours; and if we will have God to remit our former sins, we must beware that we do not willingly sin against His Majesty afresh, but that we strive against temptation to come" (Bishop Lancelot Andrewes, *Ninety-six Sermons*, 441).
67. Ibid., 93.
68. Church Catechism, *The Book of Common Prayer* (1928), http://justus.anglican.org/resources/bcp/1928/Catechism.htm.
69. Isaac Barrow, *The Works of Isaac Barrow, D.D.*, vol. 3, 10–11.
70. The Lord's Prayer is introduced twice into the order of the administration of the Lord's Supper; and a comparison between the two different parts of the office in which the prayer is found will serve to illustrate the care with which every part of the liturgy has been prepared. At the commencement of the Communion office, the Lord's Prayer is, according to the pattern contained in the gospel by Luke, without the doxology. But, when repeated in the post-Communion, immediately after the distribution of the sacred elements, the doxology is subjoined, according to the gospel by Matthew. As if the compilers of our prayer book would thus remind us that the sacrifice of praise to the "HOLY, HOLY, HOLY, Lord God of Hosts" (*The Book of Common Prayer* [1928]), whose is *"the kingdom, the power, and the glory, for ever"* (Matthew 6:13), will best be performed by those whose souls have been strengthened and refreshed by the body and blood of Christ at His holy table! In like manner, the doxology is not subjoined to the Lord's Prayer either in the office of baptism or in the order of confirmation; but it seems to be purposely reserved for those who, in the sacrament of the Lord's Supper, publicly receive Him as the Bread of Life and who, at holy baptism, had received them into the congregation of His church.
71. "The power of God may be regarded as a name of the Son, and the glory of God, as a name of the Holy Ghost. And it may be, therefore, that there is some great mystery concerning the Father hidden under the word *kingdom*. In old times, the very mention of three things would have brought the most Holy Trinity to men's minds." (See *The British Critic, and Quarterly Theological Review*, vol. 26 [London: C. & J. Rivington, 1839], 93).

72. Collect for the Third Sunday in Lent, *The Book of Common Prayer* (1662), http://justus.anglican.org/resources/bcp/1662/Orig_manuscript/collects_epistles_gospels1.htm.
73. Archbishop Robert Leighton.
74. Collect for the Eleventh Sunday After Trinity, *The Book of Common Prayer* (1662), http://justus.anglican.org/resources/bcp/1662/Orig_manuscript/collects_epistles_gospels2.htm.
75. Archbishop Robert Leighton.
76. Robert Leighton, *The Whole Works f the Most Reverend Father in God, Robert Leighton, D.D., Archbishop of Glasgow*, vol. 1 (London: 1828), 535.
77. Collect at the Holy Communion, *The Book of Common Prayer* (1928), http://justus.anglican.org/resources/bcp/1928/HC.htm.
78. Collect in the Post-Communion, *The Book of Common Prayer* (1928), http://justus.anglican.org/resources/bcp/1928/HC.htm.
79. "Herewith the prayer ends, by leaving the image of eternity before us" (Augustus William Hare, *The Alton Sermons*, 485).
80. Prayer of Saint Chrysostom quoted in *The Book of Common Prayer* (1789), http://justus.anglican.org/resources/bcp/1789Selections/MP&EP.htm.
81. Jeremy Taylor, *The Golden Grove: A Choice Manual, Containing What Is to Be Believed, Practised, and Desired, or Prayed For; The Prayers Being Fitted to the Several Days of the Week* (London: 1870), 72–82.
82. It will be seen that, in paraphrasing this clause of the Lord's Prayer, "*Give us this day our daily bread,*" Bishop Jeremy Taylor views it only as relating to the supply of our bodily wants; but, in the exposition of the Lord's Prayer, which he gives in Part 2, "History of the Life and Death of the Holy Jesus," of his book *The Whole Works of the Right Rev. Jeremy Taylor, D.D*, vol. 2, he adopts the twofold interpretation which is given by the early fathers and which is so well expressed in our Church Catechism, by "all things that are needful both for our souls and bodies" (*The Book of Common Prayer* [1928]). In the abovementioned exposition, after giving the first and most obvious interpretation of the clause, the bishop proceeds as follows: "There is also a Bread which came down from heaven, a diviner nutriment of our souls, the food and wine of angels, Christ Himself, as He communicates Himself in His word and sacraments. And if we be destitute of this Bread, we are miserable and perishing people. We must pray, therefore, that our souls may feed upon that heavenly food, prepared for us during our pilgrimage upon earth, till the great and fuller meal of the supper of the Lamb shall answer all our prayers and satisfy every desire." (See Jeremy Taylor, *The Whole Works of the Right Rev. Jeremy Taylor, D.D.*, vol. 3 [London: 1851], 227.)
83. See Samuel Ogden, *Sermons by Samuel Ogden* (London: 1832), 71–74.
84. The Order for the Administration of the Lord's Supper or Holy Communion, *The Book of Common Prayer* (1928), http://justus.anglican.org/resources/bcp/1928/HC.htm.

ABOUT THE AUTHOR

The Rev. Robert Anderson (1792–1843) served as perpetual curate of Trinity Chapel in Brighton, England.

Even as a young boy, "he walked in all the simplicity of the gospel," said his widow, Caroline D. Anderson, who published a book of his letters and thoughts on his life in 1849. "He had early imbibed that pure and heavenly tone of mind which invariably received good and rejected evil."

Left in the care of relatives while his father was stationed in India, "he was remarkable for his conscientious adherence to all their injunctions," she wrote. "When he used to pass part of his holidays with his great uncle, Bishop Douglas of Salisbury, it was his invariable remark that his little nephew was the best behaved boy he ever saw, and he would hold him up for example to others."

Coming from a wealthy family, Anderson was first educated at the exclusive Harrow School in London, but "extremely delicate health" and "increasing illness" forced him to withdraw. He then attended Haileybury and Imperial Service College near Hertford, England, and joined the Madras Civil Service in India upon graduation.

When his father died and his mother returned to England, Anderson felt it was his duty to remain in India. At the death of one of his brothers in 1818, he left his post for a short time to be with his family. However, "the dangerous state of his health" caused him to remain in England for good.

"His return to India would have been certain death," Mrs. Anderson wrote. "The medical friends who attended him in London considered the disease which eventually proved fatal to him to have then begun." While she never states what plagued her husband, it is clear that he suffered poor health for much of his life.

Anderson briefly served as assistant professor of oriental languages at East India College in Haileybury before being ordained as an Episcopal deacon in 1821 and then as a priest the following year. In 1825, he purchased Trinity Chapel in Brighton, which was consecrated by the Bishop of Chichester on April 21, 1826, with Anderson as its minister and perpetual curate.

Anderson wed his wife, Caroline Dorothea, the daughter of John Shore, the First Baron Teignmouth, in Marylebone Church on February 12, 1829. They had five children.

In addition to *The Lord's Prayer: A Manual of Religious Knowledge*, Anderson wrote *A Practical Exposition of the Gospel According to St. John*, *A Practical Exposition of St. Paul's Epistle to the Romans*, *Ten Discourses on the Communion Office of the Church of England*, *Discourses on the Beatitudes*, *A Pastoral Address on Regeneration*, *The Book of Common Prayer: A Manual of Christian Fellowship*, and *The Christian Planted Together with Christ.*